Blokes & **boats**

Blokes & boats

text Bill McCarthy ‖ photography Brian Moorhead

HarperCollins*Publishers (New Zealand) Limited*

First published 2000

Reprinted 2000

HarperCollins*Publishers (New Zealand) Limited*

P.O. Box 1, Auckland

ISBN 1 86950 330 9

Designed and typeset by jandesign. Jan Harris/Ian Gwilt

Printed by Brebner Print, Auckland

Acknowledgements

One of the most pleasant tasks I had, during putting this book together, was travelling from the far north of New Zealand to the far south. During these journeys I discovered, or rediscovered, some of the most beautiful places on this planet. Sometimes it took me many hours of driving just to obtain a solitary interview, others required a reasonably long sea journey to track down that elusive bloke. For the driving segment I thank Ford NZ for providing me with a vehicle. For the maritime journeys thanks are due to my old and close friend Wal Edwards, who found nothing too much trouble. Thanks also to my wife Rae, who spent so many hours on the phone and at the fax machine during her own busy schedule, trying to seek out these people, and who kept me going when things got tough. I thank my daughters, Rachael and Julia, who spent hours trying to decipher my nearly unintelligible handwriting. And special thanks to Brian Moorhead, the photographer, who has that amazing skill that few possess — the ability to create a photograph with that angle or look to it that makes all the difference. And finally I thank the contributors themselves, who were gracious with their time and their memories. The stories in this book are not long, but I hope that I have captured something of the essence of their love affair with boats and the sea.

Bill McCarthy

Introduction

With boats there appear to be no grey areas. It's all black or white — you either like or dislike. For each of the people I spoke to during the preparation of this book — and I spoke to hundreds — lurking unseen in the background there were people, both men and women, who couldn't stand the thought of boats. It's not necessarily all one-way traffic either, although I must say that those on the distaff side tended to be the ones who thought that boating was tedious, time-wasting, expensive nonsense.

And now I've dealt with the negative, how about some positive?

In my 40 years of professional life I have interviewed literally thousands of people, and produced and directed thousands of television items. But rarely, before researching this book, had I come across a group of individuals so dedicated to what I would describe as the crux, the core, the quintessence of love of boats and the sea.

I travelled from Kerikeri to Bluff talking to all sorts of folk about their passionate relationships with boats. Clearly some were more ardent than others, but all had some sort of instinctive in-built barometer that registered 'hot' when the topic of boats was broached.

Take someone like Peter Richards out of Opua. He speaks of his boat *Undine* as if she were one of the family — which she surely is. In reality she looks rather rough — beaten-up, some might say — but the passion with which Peter describes this much-loved child is enough to move even the harshest critic.

At the other end of the country, Jack Crooks' lean-to shed houses only the barest essentials of what was clearly once a very fine vessel, *Southern Light*. What a valiant effort it takes to bring such a broken craft back to life. There is a confidence, a certainty, an arrogance almost, that treats these hurdles as mere bagatelles; there is absolutely no doubt in Jack's mind that *Southern Light* will rise

from the wrecker's grasp and once again whisper out of port on the morning breeze and tide.

Most of the stories are not of restoration, although these do comprise a sizeable portion; in the main these stories are concerned with the living, breathing ships that adorn the coast. Not all are old, but many are. Not all are sailboats, but most are. And the rest — the steamboats and launches that fill out this volume — are all part of the proud tradition of ownership that prompted the ideas for this book in the first place.

Delving far back to the turn of last century has been the most fascinating aspect of this whole adventure. The Logans and the Baileys, famous then for their design and building genius and still famous 100 years on, put to water some of the most exquisite maritime creations known to man. Combining their phenomenal techniques, the glorious patch that is the northern cruising waters of New Zealand, the enthusiasm of the participants and the

kauri tree — the essence of all great New Zealand wooden boats — the scene was set a century ago for the nurturing of the inherent skill, daring and knowledge that won us an America's Cup.

My admiration for the pioneers then — through from Col Wild, the Lidgards, Max Carter, Jim Davern, Roy Dickson, Laurie Davidson and Des Townson through to Sir Tom Clarke, Sir Peter Blake and hundreds of others — is boundless. Not all are in this book. These stories speak for themselves and are only a fraction of the treasure trove of tales awaiting discovery. I have chosen 50 for this book. There are at least another 100 waiting to be told.

This book is dedicated to all those who go down to the sea in ships.

Bill McCarthy

Brett_{Avery}

Brett Avery is not being boastful when he claims to be a good, maybe even great, designer and builder of gizmos. 'They ask me to do all sorts of things for big American movies,' he confides.

The latest project is some rafts for the film company DreamWorks. The movie is *Castaway*, starring Tom Hanks, and is to be shot in the Islands. 'I got the poplar and willow off Te Horo beach and took everything to California. They don't have driftwood up there.' Is this the boat I have associated with this bloke? 'No, no. I do have a real boat, and she's a beauty.' Her name is *Caprice*, and she was built in Sweden in 1930 for some English owners. She was raced extensively in the northern hemisphere before being shipped to New Zealand. 'Chris Bouzaid owned her, and so did Alan Martin of L.V. Martin fame, but at that time she was named *Shirleen*. She's also been called *Reimers*, and at one time *Cherie*.'

The path from the New Plymouth lad's early sailing experiences to finally owning *Caprice* is typical of that followed by so many Kiwi boaties. P-class, Zeddies, Javelins followed by a boating hiatus when the need to earn a living — as a design consultant, industrial designer and model-maker — became paramount. 'I thought I'd finished with yachting,' he admits. 'Then, one day, I saw *Shirleen* in Wellington. I bought her the next day.' That was in 1976.

Much was to happen before *Caprice* got to where she is today. Racing out of Wellington one dark and stormy night, Brett headed her into Tasman Bay, cut the corner, bounced over the reef at high speed, tore a hole in the bottom and sank her in 60 feet of water. When he got her up and took a good look at her, he saw there was plenty to be done besides repairing the damage from the accident. 'The steel ribs had caused chemical decay. There was rot, and the boat was bent upwards forward of the mast.' Nothing a few thousand hours of hard work wouldn't fix. Under a tent of tarpaulins in Matauwhi Bay, the long slog was on. 'I estimated six months,' he says. 'It took four years!'

A strange reminder of *Caprice*'s northern-heritage origins came during this time. Peter Taylor, of the English Square Rig Association, was searching for a 30-metre square-rig vessel he knew to be in New Zealand. Someone told him of a long, narrow boat hiding under the trees in Matauwhi Bay — and, lo, the lost yacht was found. Come 1996, a huge crowd sipped wine and beer as the graceful vessel — fully restored and once more bearing her original name — was returned to the water. From Brett's elevated property in the Bay of Islands, we gaze down at *Caprice* as she swings at anchor. 'Got to go now. We're racing in an hour.' Brett heads off to the mooring. *Caprice* has to earn her keep.

Mark_{Baxter}

The Baxters have had a presence in the Marlborough Sounds for over 100 years. Bert Baxter, the patriarch, was born in Te Weka Bay on a property bounded by a whalebone fence — a practical and, in those days, plentiful material. After he shifted to Picton, he started building boats.

His son, Buddy Baxter, born in Picton, kept the family flag flying. He also capitalised on a glorious opportunity. The frequent ferry services between Wellington and Picton in the early 1960s led to the steady opening-up of the Sounds, and the owners of baches accessible only by boat needed a means of getting to and fro. Enter the water taxi.

Sea Bud, both designed and built by A.S. Baxter, the family firm, was the first and, for years, the fastest sea taxi in the Sounds. Sure, there were plenty of launches, but nothing as swift as *Sea Bud*. A Ford Thunderbird V8 engine got you where you needed to be in double quick time.

Enter next Mark Baxter — Buddy's son. He first held the the helm of *Sea Bud* at age seven. The Picton waterfront has been his patch ever since.

In the mid-1960s Mark had a fleet of small dinghies with old Seagull outboards that he rented to adventurous passers-by. This involved high finance. Working capital was raised by selling Coke and beer bottles (they were worth something in those days) and copper nails scrounged from boat-building yards. Mark also collected 2-cent pieces from the floors of telephone boxes.

'You wouldn't believe how much I made from those telephone boxes,' he laughs. 'People dropped coins in the dark and didn't bother looking for them.'

When Buddy retired in 1990, Mark took over the water-taxi business. The number of ferries they run has increased, but so has the competition. *Sea Bud* is still in service but there have been additions to the family. *Sea Bud 2* in 1967. *Sea Bud 3* in 1970. All roughly the same design, but the focus has changed. Fishing charters and police transfers are now entered in the log book.

Who knows how many trips the *Sea Bud*s have made, how many passengers they've hauled round the Sounds? Mark has the Sounds in his blood. 'There's nowhere else like it. We love it here.'

If you're down that way and looking for a ride, just keep an eye out for *Sea Bud* — it's first away from the rank. And by the way, that's Mark's three-year-old son, Hamish, at the wheel.

John Bolland

John Bolland built his first boat when he was 13.

'I did the whole lot for twenty-seven pounds, seven shillings and sixpence. That was a lot of money in 1946. I got a sail from Leo Bouzaid — that cost me five pounds.'

Wakatere was John's early stamping ground, where fellow yachties always lent a helping hand and supplied each other with whatever bits and pieces they could.

'Frostbites were the go — we used to race without life jackets in all weathers. Mind you, everyone did — absolutely fearless we were.'

John always wanted to be a boat-builder, but the great Jack Brooke had a strong point of view on that.

'"It's a boom game, it won't last," he used to tell me. "If you want to do something smart with your hands, be a cabinet-maker."'

Which John has now been for 52 years.

'I remember, though, in Jim Young's boat yard in Barry's Point Road in Takapuna, this excited young guy saying to me, "I've just designed my first boat."'

The young guy's name was Bruce Farr.

'About thirty-five years ago I started dabbling in model boats. I made a mould and put it away for twenty-eight years. But I still did full-sized boats as well.'

He shows me a Boston whaler in the garage.

'That hull is thirty-five years old. It's had five outboards, and I've raced it in the old Epiglass Forty regatta. It's as good as ever.' He thumps it to demonstrate.

But back to the models.

'I built a free-sailing one, and that's really where it all started. I've made a replica Canadian Bluenose schooner of 1920s vintage, and now I'm working on a modification of that.'

His early models have since been inherited by his grandsons, whose appreciation of his workmanship is a source of great pleasure.

It takes John about six months to build a boat. All round the house are reminders of his maritime expertise: a sail jig downstairs next to the door, partially completed models, photographs, mementos.

John is also an active member of the Ancient Mariners, that trusty band of radio-controlled-yacht enthusiasts who frequent Onepoto Lake, on Auckland's North Shore, every Thursday — weather permitting, of course.

'Come and join us. It's all fun,' says John. 'It's great to see the classic designs and craft the members come up with.'

The invitation is sincere, and I do.

There is something therapeutic about the experience. It also requires skill, and although I say it myself, I'm not bad. Wanna see the home video?

David Bott

It was no great surprise that the neighbours became a little cheesed off with the trimaran in David Bott's front garden. The property in the Auckland suburb of Epsom is small; the trimaran hull isn't. But how did the boat get there in the first place? And what happened to it?

As a boy, David enjoyed messing around in fizz boats with his father.

'But it was really a trip on the *Spirit of Adventure* when I was in sixth form that gave me a taste for sailing.'

He bought the classic starter boat, a Hartley 16-foot trailer sailer, and the world, he says, 'opened up'.

'But a day sail in 1981 turned to custard when the boat capsized north of Whangamata. We were picked up after one and a half hours in the water, and the boat was retrieved two days later, thirty miles offshore — next stop, Chile.'

To this day, whenever David goes sailing, he has a well-stocked grab bag at the ready.

In July 1985, *Pickety Witch*, a 38-foot trimaran, was David's next purchase (he still has her). Extensive cruising was the favourite activity for the next nine years. Then, in the mid 1990s, he saw a partly constructed main hull of a Piver AA 36 trimaran and immediately had thoughts of finishing it off and sailing into the sunset. Thus began the saga of the hull, the lawn and the neighbours. Remember,

it was a big boat and a small lawn.

'I actually had to cut the handrails off the steps to fit the beams into the boat,' David chuckles.

Four years' work followed. The cabin and the wheelhouse were constructed and the interior of the main hull built in Epsom; the floats were constructed at David's parents' property in Paeroa.

The end of May 1997 was the date promised by David to the neighbours for removal of the boat from the property. All the pieces were transported to Okahu Bay, where another year was spent assembling *Pengwen*. 27 May 1998 was launching day.

'I cried,' admits David. 'I was just so damned emotional.'

What now?

'I'd like to sail under Tower Bridge, cruise the Caribbean, cross the Pacific . . .'

That dream of sailing off into the sunset might just come true. At least the neighbours won't worry David there.

Alan Brimblecombe

What is it about steam power? There can be few people more passionate about their hobby than steam-railway enthusiasts. Yet no less passionate, it seems, are steamboat aficionados. Alan Brimblecombe is one of them.

Alan's affair with steam began when he was a young boy in Paeroa, which was at that time a notable inland port. Everything was steam then. Steamboats reigned supreme, ranging from two to 200 tonnes. Like all steamboat men, Alan's eyes light up when anyone talks steam, and over the years he and his wife, Zelma, have owned 14 boats of consequence, and restored several.

Alan has made many coastal passages and penetrations inland by waterways of yesteryear, from which the little commercial steamers have long since vanished. *Zeltic* is his current steamer. She's an old boat, made in 1903 to be exact, and like so many vessels of that era she's undergone numerous modifications over the years. She came from the Lanes yard at Totara North, and was originally a motor vessel. In 1990, Alan spied her, much the worse for wear, in the Waiheke mangroves, rotting away as a converted gaff-rigged cutter.

Zeltic is 25 feet long and built of kauri, with a turn-of-the-century A.G. Price steam engine — to be precise, a vertical, single-cylinder, double-acting, reversing marine engine. A straight-stem, triple-skin vessel, *Zeltic* has received many brass and traditional refinements, including a large colourful plated and riveted funnel which exhales the aromatic coal smoke from the furnace of the vertical fire tube boiler below.

But *Zeltic*'s no show pony. In the winter of 1994, with a friend, Alan completed the 'long voyage', a 430 nautical mile excursion up the Thames River, past Paeroa, Te Aroha and Stanley's Landing, in the wake of the great steam voyages of last century. They slept snug and smug beneath the frosted decks near the well-banked boiler; the furnace always provided means for the instant cooking of breakfasts on those cold mornings.

Alan has a reputation for converting boats into steamers and for having steamed more miles than anyone else, in new or restored boats, in the last half of the 20th century in this part of the world. In his inimitable jocular fashion, Alan scorns diesel- and petrol-powered vessels. 'Diseasilised' is a word he's invented, and he makes dark references to the 'infernal combustion engine'. He prefers the long plumes of aromatic smoke and the thud and pump of the steam engine, the comfort of a sedate and leisurely pace.

'I'm a life member of the Auckland Steamship Society.' Alan is clearly proud of that distinction. 'I'm really grateful for the fellowship of steamboat men.'

With Alan at the helm, *Zeltic* has many more voyages to complete and many more miles to run.

John Chibnall

When the subject of big-game fishing in the Bay of Islands comes up, I immediately think of Zane Grey. Grey was an American who wrote Westerns and thought the Bay of Islands was paradise on earth. I'm sitting in the Paihia Swordfishing Club, talking to John Chibnall. The subject of our conversation is *Otehei* — not the bay, but the boat.

'Zane Grey commissioned a sporting club at Otehei Bay and wanted four boats built,' explains John. 'They were *Zane Grey*, *Manaki*, *Lorna Doone* and *Otehei*.

'These vessels were turned out by Collings and Bell, a well-known Auckland firm of the time.

'They were built to a tried and tested whale-chaser design . . . very fast. Those original whale-chasers could clock eighteen knots,' John explains.

The boats eventually went off in different directions, and to all intents and purposes *Otehei* was lost. Then, in 1976, she resurfaced — in Taupo, of all places. She'd been there 30 years. The shape looked familiar, but the name was *Rangitira*. Where the paint was scraped off, there was the original name, *Otehei*, etched in the woodwork. John bought the boat, having decided she was worth putting back together.

'We did what we could,' he says, 'but felt she wasn't quite what we wanted.' *Otehei*, then as now, was run by a trust, and there was much discussion about her future.

'Gavin Bradley, Bill Reece and Terry Hancox, members of the trust, had put in a lot of work, and together we decided she deserved another go at restoration.'

Craig McInnes, of Opua, took on the job, which proved a real mission. The original bolts were iron and had deteriorated badly. But the hull was basically sound — three cheers for kauri. Glassed over, *Otehei* is now in magnificent trim.

'She's not for the museum,' John reassures me. 'We wanted to use her, and we do. We take out people who genuinely enjoy old boats. She's not as fast as the original designs — a comfortable eleven knots these days.'

John has a word or two about game fishing, — he's done plenty. 'We're actually the watchdogs of the sea. We catch and release. The Atlantic is fished out — they take marlin commercially there. In fact, marlin are taken commercially in most places.'

Otehei is moored just off the Opua wharf, gleaming like a new pin.

'We do fish her from here,' says John, gazing at her wistfully. 'Last year we landed three marlin.'

Zane Grey would be well pleased.

Sir Thomas Clark

Surprisingly, the only boat Sir Thomas Clark owns at the moment is a small aluminium runabout he uses to catch the odd fish. So where does he fit into the world of blokes and boats? The answer comes in two words: *Infidel* and *Buccaneer*. Sir Thomas's association with these two vessels is more than sufficient to raise the big man into any New Zealand boating hall of fame.

Once you meet Tom Clark, you never forget him. His voice thunders with a foghorn quality. And he tells it like it is. As someone once said of him: 'He calls a spade a ten-ton digger.'

'I had the best childhood a kid could ever have. I was brought up in Hobsonville, with acres to muck around in next to the water's edge. In 1931, at the age of fourteen, I began work at Amalgamated Brick and Pipe — the clay works part-owned by my father. I barrowed thirty tons a day. I was fit, and keen as mustard.' So fit he was Lyndale junior long-distance champion in 1933 and 1934.

Sir Thomas relates the steady rise of the company over which he came to preside. 'Besides bricks and pipes, the factory was soon turning out tableware. We renamed the company Crown Lynn. We had a thousand people working for us at one stage. The old building's a picture theatre now.'

Tom Clark's inexhaustible entrepreneurship was matched by his legendary recreational exploits. 'When I was thirty, I bought myself a boat and taught myself to sail.' For more excitement he went motor racing. 'I entered my Super Squallo Ferrari in the 1957 Australian Grand Prix, but when I ended up underneath it after a particularly bad crash, I decided it was getting too exciting,' he chuckles.

So it was back to yachting. Enter *Infidel*, from the board of the late John Spencer. 'I had her built with one thing in mind: to beat *Ranger*. And she did, too, for a couple of years.'

Then, in 1970, came *Buccaneer*. 'She was another Spencer, designed for ocean racing and having a bit of fun.' His laugh is pure gravel. *Buccaneer* was sold in 1977, and the Clarks went to live at South Kaipara Heads, with a bach on Kawau Island where Tom pottered around in a Soling.

Next came *Ceramco*, Bruce Farr's round-the-world flier, built for Peter Blake and named after the international business empire. 'Could have won if she hadn't lost her mast off Africa.'

What now for Sir Tom? 'I'm on the board to help give Blakey the tools to get the America's Cup job done. Then I want to have my eighty-fifth birthday out there on the lawn.' He gestures towards the window. 'Then I'll move on.' After all those years in business, Sir Thomas Clark is at ease on the property he has handcrafted from the Kaipara backblocks. There's a huge story there. And don't worry about his fearsome reputation — his bark is worse than his bite.

Ken Clunies-Ross

Most of us have dreamt of having our boat moored at the bottom of the garden. For Ken Clunies-Ross the dream has come true — almost. His fishing boat, *Mystic*, is at the bottom of a friend's property. Which is where the daily ritual of heading seaward for the big haul begins.

It might not be Ken's land, but the setting is idyllic. The lower reaches of the Wairau River form a tidal estuary that encloses a biggish lagoon, and there, tucked under a bank of blue gums, is *Mystic*.

If the colour of a house — or, in this case, a boat — reflects its owner's personality, Ken must be an intriguing bloke. A bold brush has layered *Mystic* in primary yellow and red, a standout in any company. But don't judge a boat by its colour. Since its launch in 1950, this Jack Morgan 28-footer has passed from father to son, bits have been added, engines have come and gone, and the boat has chalked up thousands of miles. 'Customised for Ken's convenience' is a good way to describe the many changes she has undergone. Hard-to-reach bits have extensions, shaped from a variety of recycled levers.

If there is a typical South Islander, I suppose Ken could be described as one. If being a South Islander means being modest to a fault, and reluctant to talk about oneself, then Ken fits the bill exactly. I managed to get him to talk about his upbringing, albeit briefly.

'I'm a Blenheim boy actually . . . the family goes back quite a way. Dad got the boat from my grandfather — it was used as a pleasure boat. Then when I received it, I altered it to a fishing boat and became a commercial fisherman.'

There's a sand bar at the entrance to the lagoon. *Mystic* has ended up there a couple of times and had to wait for the incoming tide to float her clear. It's a constant hazard Ken negotiates every day, netting for the flatfish or red cod that find a ready market in Blenheim.

For classic Kiwi ingenuity, look no further than Ken's dinghy. This has been fashioned from a mussel-farm mooring buoy, found adrift after a storm, by cutting the heavy-duty plastic in two down the middle. Take one half, lay a piece of 4 x 2 across the middle, and hey presto — transport.

For safety purposes, I should point out it only has to travel about 6 metres out to the boat and 6 metres back. So why go to the expense of a nice fibreglass one? He's been there, wrecked that.

Mystic is a product of the days when they built 'em tough. So is Ken Clunies-Ross. A quiet soul engaged in one of the toughest professions. Ask any fisherman who ventures into Cook Strait.

Among the boats that ply the waters round the upper South Island, *Mystic* will always be a bit special — if only for her unmistakable colour scheme.

Mike Colman

There are some boats that have a shape and a presence which stay in the memory long after one's first look at them. Their names, too, can stick in the mind. Such a boat is *Lady Crossley* — so symmetrical. She isn't a Logan boat, but she is a reminder of the Logan comment: 'If a boat looks right, she is right.'

There is a definite 1940s feel to the shape, but the lines are as sweet today as they were in the designer's mind over 50 years ago. A very young Mike Colman was in the Col Wild yard with his father one day and saw the boat being built for the Seager brothers.

'I asked Dad, "Why can't we have a boat like that?" She wasn't for sale.' Then Mike made one of those delightful predictions: 'I'm going to own that boat one day.'

There were always boats around as Mike grew up, from duck punts to Finns to Cherubs. As the years rolled by, the gap between Mike and *Lady Crossley* steadily closed.

'I remember the *Lady* was an unusual boat from the start,' Mike recalls. 'When they had finished her, the builders put her on the chocks overnight for launching next day. When they arrived in the morning, she was already floating serenely in the bay. A high tide had lifted her off and she had launched herself — a very good omen.'

The guys in the yard were sweating, though.

They had only tapped the bungs in, and *Lady Crossley* could have sunk.

'Originally she was fitted with Crossley engines, as the Seagers were the agents for Crossley Marine and Aero Engines, so maybe she was the first sponsored boat in New Zealand,' offers Mike.

She was sold to Wellington owners, who used her extensively in the Sounds. Then back she came to Auckland and remained in the hands of the Sanders brothers from the 1950s to the 1980s. Mike's father-in-law tried to buy her — no deal. Then one day, out of the blue, Vic Sanders rang Mike and said she was for sale. Mike recalls a speedy trip to the wharf; surely his prediction was about to come true.

'Inside I saw she was in bad shape, and the afterdeck was rotten. I was gutted, but said no to buying her.'

Some years later Mike saw her again in Fiji, in the care of new owners. But she returned to New Zealand and Mike had another opportunity to purchase her.

'This time I bit the bullet, fulfilling my prophecy some thirty years down the track.'

The long refit followed, and *Lady Crossley* was reborn — a lady of class and character, just as Mike had seen in the Wild yard all those years before.

You will definitely see her cruising round the Hauraki Gulf and beyond — that distinctive shape, that unforgettable name.

Jack Crooks

'Welcome to the Rakiura boat yard.'

Jack Crooks has led me through the trees to a small patch of turf on Rakiura Parade, a few kilometres west of Invercargill in the general direction of Riverton. Hardly the place for a boat yard; nevertheless, a quick look round convinces me it does qualify as such — just.

Three boats are in various stages of construction or reconstruction, but 'yard'? More a tin shed with a lean-to covering the craft Jack is so passionate about.

'When I first set eyes on it I thought it was the most beautiful boat I'd ever seen,' he enthuses. 'She was built in 1934, to a design, we think, by the American William Hand, and christened *Southern Light*. The Invercargill builders were tremendously resourceful. They cut wood out of the local bush and used obsolete gig shafts for her inner frames.'

Variously a yacht and a fishing boat out of Riverton, *Southern Light* was once a common sight around the southern waters of Foveaux Strait. It was just up the coast, near Tuatapere, that she came to grief. Dragging her anchor she went aground and became stranded. Her hull holed, her totara planking ripped, she seemed beyond repair. The situation didn't improve when the bulldozer charged with retrieving the hulk pulled the stern clean out as it dragged her over the rocks.

Jack spied a tender notice for the wreck in a local paper, rekindling an interest he had had as an admirer some 30 years before. But, his tender successful, he found himself the proud owner of only the saddest reminder of the boat's former self. So why did Jack buy the thing?

'I really loved her,' he declares. 'But then the enormity of the restoration task hit me. There were no plans or drawings, yet I really wanted to see her sail again.' Smart detective work uncovered a 1923 *American Rudder* magazine and there, spread over several pages, was what had to be the plans of *Southern Light*. 'The lines look right although the rig is different, so the builders must have added their own touches to the original plan,' Jack figures, poring over the old drawings. With his unstoppable enthusiasm, he is now on the job.

The mind boggles at the sheer audacity of it. And there are so many others like him, who have taken on the awesome task of rebuilding boats — usually vintage vessels with a complex architecture.

'I've built a large yacht and sailed round the world already — this is what I want to do now,' concludes Jack. 'I've seen photos of the gaff ketch in its original state, and there's no doubt it was a classic.' It does look quite forlorn at the moment. It's hard to imagine that Jack can ever reincarnate this vessel, but never underestimate the tenacity of a Southlander. When she sails again, *Southern Light* will be a sight to behold.

Jim Davern

I have never heard Jim Davern and Sir Tom Clark in conversation. Why do I mention this? Because it would be a contest for Most Gravelly Voice of Our Times. Both have a lilting foghorn quality that is quite unmistakable. As it happens, the two men are good friends, so I await the day when they exchange words in my presence. But I digress.

Jim Davern — who is he?

In 1967, skippering a yacht called *Fidelis*, he stunned Australians and delighted New Zealanders by winning the Sydney–Hobart race.

'When we got back to New Zealand and came around North Head, there were thousands of people out in boats and lining the roadways. It was bloody emotional — after all, we'd only won a boat race.'

But that single maritime triumph arguably launched New Zealand on its way to its current pre-eminence as a yachting nation. Did it lead to the America's Cup? It certainly woke people up to the possibility of international competitiveness.

Jim Davern is someone everybody seems to know. He has proved he can foot it with the best and mostly come out on top.

At the age of seven he built a canoe at Auckland's Point Chevalier. Then he dug a P-class out of the sand. Zeddies followed, then an Idle-along. 'I was beaten by Peter Mander in the 1951 nationals,' he recalls. 'He went on to win the gold medal.'

Stewart 34s were Jim's chosen sailing boats, and he did spectacularly well in them, especially *Princess*, which he had built in 1959. But the best was yet to come.

'I was up at Kawau, and *Fidelis* was in the bay. Vic Speight had her built for one reason only — to beat *Ranger*. I went over to Vic and told him I wanted to buy her. I had no money but I convinced him I could get the better of *Ranger*. "OK," said Vic. "You beat *Ranger*, you can have her."'

So around Waiheke they sailed — *Ranger* versus *Fidelis*. Eleven hours later, line honours went to *Fidelis* by 11 seconds. The graceful yacht and Jim Davern have been an item ever since.

'In 1967, when I took her to Sydney, they said, "What are you going to do with that drainpipe?" Let the records speak for themselves.'

There was also a period when Jim raced mulleties. 'Get a dozen of beer and a packet of cheese, and sit under a table for a week. It's the same,' was his father's sage advice. But Jim built his own mullet boat, *Honey*, won the single-race Lipton Cup, then sold her. Another feather in his sailor's cap.

What else? Oh, just Yachtsman of the Year, third place in New Zealand Sportsman of the Year, owned a hugely successful house-moving business, now spends six months of the year in Fiji on his yacht, *Cobalt*.

'Beat that for a lifestyle,' he challenges me.

I can't. Jim Davern, quite simply, is a winner.

Roy Dickson

Roy Dickson is Chris Dickson's father — let's clear that up right away. But although Chris might be the famous one — America's Cup, Whitbread Round the World and all — here's the brief story of a remarkable yachtsman.

'I was born and bred on the mud of Shoal Bay, on Auckland's North Shore. Vic Lidgard, Chris Robertson, Jim Young, Jim and Don Lidgard — they all came out of Northcote like me. Remember where the Auckland Harbour Bridge tollgates used to be?' (For those who don't, it was where the motorway flattens out coming off the bridge to the north.) 'That's Sulphur Beach — all the old boats were left there to rot. We got all sorts of bits and pieces from them.' From 1955–57 Roy, his brother and father built a 43-foot keeler called *Tuahine*. The planks were caulked — a dying art even then.

'*Ranger* was the top boat then, and the three of us crewed on her. It was a Tercel-Dickson team.'

It can be argued that international keel-boat racing began with *Fidelis* winning the Sydney–Hobart in 1967. When Chris Bouzaid's *Rainbow Two* won the One Ton Cup in Heligoland in 1969, with Roy Dickson a member of the crew, New Zealand was really on the international yachting map.

'A remarkable win that spurred New Zealand keel-boat building into action.'

Roy was also on *Moonlight*, the Townson 32-footer that nearly caused a sensation in the 1971 One Ton Cup trials. Then, when 1975 rolled around, he was on *45 South*, which brought home the world quarter-ton trophy. And so he continued as a crew member on a succession of high-performance boats — *Tempo, Red Lion, Wee Willie Winkie, Jumpin' Jack Flash*.

'I was appointed team coach for the 1980 Olympics in Russia — you'll recall we didn't go.'

In his versatility Roy is the classic Kiwi yachtsman, sailing everything in the range from M-class to Maxis. Management is another strength. He helped set up the Japanese challenge for the 1992 America's Cup in San Diego. Seven years later he helped the Swiss set up camp in Auckland. 'Let's just say that everything about the America's Cup management was a learning experience.' Roy's wide grin, when I press for details, reveals that there is more to this story than he is telling.

His friendship with Chris Bouzaid continues. 'I sail in the States with him from time to time — he's as fiercely competitive as ever.'

He could be talking about himself. Today, still looking as young and fit as ever, he actively campaigns his Stewart 34 and sails on *Starlight Express*.

The boy from the mud in Shoal Bay has done it all. In fact, he's forgotten more about sailing than most people ever learn.

Terry Dunn

In the magnificent *Southern Breeze: A history of yachting in New Zealand*, she is introduced thus: 'In November came *Aorere*, built by Robert Logan Senior for Tom Kitfoyle, former owner of *Tangaroa*.'

The *Observer* declared *Aorere* one of the handsomest craft turned out in Auckland, and the *New Zealand Herald* enthused: 'She has a remarkable turn of speed and can pass anything on the harbour.'

The year was 1892, and the Logans were at their brilliant best — as *Aorere* clearly demonstrates. But those who know, know: there are some boats that just hijack your life.

'I was looking around for one of the old Logans or Baileys — one of the classics — but they were all too expensive. Then I saw *Aorere* in Totara North sitting at the end of the jetty.

'A boat-builder had done a lot of work on the hull but the cabin and decks were fairly decayed, so I pulled her to bits to see how she was built.'

Aorere was constructed with all the finesse the Logans were able to bring to their craft at that time. The storm in 1968 that wrecked *Wahine* in Wellington Harbour nearly saw her off. She broke free of her mooring, drifted under the Evans Bay wharf and, with the pounding of wind and waves, her stern snapped off and down she went.

Terry was 10 then, and can remember seeing her submerged against the breakwater. Little did he realise that he would purchase *Aorere* in 1980. Old-timers like *Aorere*, although soundly constructed, take a long time to bring back to life — especially when you're not a boat builder.

But there usually comes a time when those who have dedicated their lives to restoring a vintage vessel can declare their labour of love complete. For Terry that was in 1990, when he and his partner took *Aorere* on an eight-month cruise to Tonga and Fiji.

'I think she's the oldest boat to have left New Zealand.' He could be right. *Waitangi*, for instance, is two years younger.

'It got a bit breezy and we had to nurse her along. I knew the drill because I'd read every book by Hiscock and Illingworth. I just kept asking myself what they would do.'

Today, *Aorere* is in Opua, not far from where Terry runs his charter business.

'I've got fourteen boats and I can maintain them a lot easier than *Aorere*. But she's got such a great feel — people really appreciate that these days.'

It's nearly 110 years since the *Observer* remarked on her good looks, yet here *Aorere* is looking much the same as in 1892, gaff rig and all.

There's warmth in Terry's final assessment: 'Ships like this usually take up part of your life. *Aorere* contributes a lot to mine.'

Norman Firth

I was once told the mark of an all-rounder was that they went to a rugby match in the afternoon and a symphony concert at night. How about crewing on *Spirit of New Zealand* during the day and singing in the Dorian Choir in the evening?

The Firth family has had a place on Lake Rotoiti for many years, and it was on the lake that Norman Firth learned to sail.

The Firths' pride and joy is a small clinker dinghy Norman's father built in 1948.

'It used to be a part of a bridge,' explains Norman, which gives new meaning to the old saying about a boat sailing like a wharf. 'It's beautiful — Squadron class, actually — and we keep it well maintained.

'When Dad launched it, he decided to take her about four or five kilometres around the lake. Halfway round up came a brisk sou'wester. The boat was leaking like a sieve and we had no life jackets. On reflection, we were lucky to make it ashore. That taught me a bit.'

As a consulting engineer, Norman has travelled to Manila and Hong Kong.

'I raced fairly extensively out of both clubs. That was a bit of a laugh.'

He hasn't raced a lot since his Manila days, but he takes great pleasure in digging out a photo of a delightful Townson 34 called *Amaryllis*.

'She's owned by my wife, Jenny, and her brother and we cruise the Gulf in her a lot. She's a great boat.'

But it's when we talk about *Spirit of New Zealand* that Norman leans forward.

'To watch those kids — some of whom have never dried a dish or cleaned up in their lives — come together as a team is one of the great joys.' Norman has been part of the volunteer crew for five years.

'I've always loved square riggers . . . there's a fascination that can't be explained. I also like the idea of a big, powerful vessel as opposed to a cruising yacht. I watch the disabled kids, the underprivileged ones and the smart ones. The *Spirit* certainly levels them out.'

It seems she also moves in mysterious ways through other parts of Norman's life. He has been an organist at Takapuna Methodist Church for 20 years and has been in and out of the Dorian Choir for 30.

Can we take a photo of the bridge turned dinghy?

'Certainly. It's over at Dad's place.'

Dad is now 96. He remembers sailing on the Logan boats when they were new, all those years ago. I wonder if he remembers the no-lifejacket leaking dinghy, in Rotoiti, with a son hanging on as they battled that sou'wester.

I'll bet he does.

Jim Francis

The 1941 photograph clearly shows a depth charge on the stern and a machine gun on the cabin roof. Jim Francis is, by his own admission, 'no spring chicken'; he has the photograph album open and is leafing through the fading prints of an era long gone. With a sprightly gleam in his eye and a rapier-sharp memory, Jim recounts the days of tough sailing.

No namby-pamby gin palace, this, but a real man o' war — well, almost. Like so many vessels of the time, national service took precedence over leisure in the early 1940s and *Lady Margaret* was 'taken up' defending the New Zealand coast.

'Honestly, I don't know what they expected to do with the depth charge — there wouldn't be a chance against, say, a submarine.'

Her life began in 1939, when Ted Clark commissioned Dick Laing to build her. She was completed on request from the navy in 1940 so she could join the Naval Auxiliary Patrol.

Remarkably, the bulky 43-footer was built from a single kauri log from Great Barrier Island. Under naval command she serviced lighthouses and was given the formidable task of intercepting incoming vessels to inform them of the location of minefields. The depth charge and machine gun provided muscle in case of an encounter of the first kind.

Jim Francis, a furniture retailer from Otahuhu, first met *Lady Margaret* in 1953, and he became her owner in 1970. It has been a happy partnership ever since. Jim has spent a lifetime on the sea, owning 26 boats since his childhood beginnings with crude corrugated-iron creations. A longtime member of Otahuhu Sailing Club, he is a true sailing veteran with the tales to prove it.

Lady Margaret has been involved in numerous rescue and tow operations, some quite sensational. She towed a boat named *Blitzen* home once after *Blitzen* was stranded on rocks at Tutukaka. Ted Clark used her to rescue an injured man from Kuvier Lighthouse in the 1940s. The weather that day was so wild that waves broke the boat's front windows — Ted ripped up the carpet and stuffed it into the window frames to keep the sea out.

Lady Margaret has the classic bridge-decker lines, and Jim has tried to maintain many of her original features. The original crockery is still in use, and the radio remains exactly as it was when installed in 1939.

Teak and oak are the vessel's principle timbers. Stepping inside, you are immediately transported back to an earlier era, before fibreglass and modern composites. Even the smell stirs waves of nostalgia.

'We probably don't use her as much as we should, but we've caught a lot of fish off her.'

With wife Nan, Jim still cruises the Hauraki Gulf on *Lady Margaret*, 60 years after she was launched — minus depth charge and machine gun, of course.

Percy Ginders

'**When I** bought *Romp* I was ridiculed because of her condition. People suggested that burning her would be the best option. But I thought, "She's worth doing up, even if I only get five years' fun out of her."'

Percy Ginders was recalling events of 30 years ago. 'Some people like vintage cars, planes or tractors. For me, it's boats.'

Anyone who has crossed paths with Percy knows that to be the understatement of the year. On his sprawling property just north of Whangarei are at least six boats, of various vintages, all precious and all marked for restoration.

Even to the untrained eye and those with only a modicum of historic boating knowledge, *Romp* would probably say 'Logan' within five seconds of coming into view. The builders of some of the greatest boats ever to sail New Zealand waters have clearly put their stamp on this 25-foot steamer. Robert Logan Senior designed and built her in the mid-1880s for an owner whose name has not been recorded. In fact, little is known about the first 25 years of her life. Then Soljack and Rosenfeldt bought her to tow barges of flax to Mount Maunganui. Like so many other little boats *Romp* also did great work around Matakana Island in Tauranga, for the Salvation Army, ferrying people and supplies to numerous outposts.

Percy came into contact with her when, as a boy in Tauranga in 1942, he used to play on board, little knowing that one day she would be his pride and joy. That day came in 1969, but the pride and joy were tinged with frustration.

'She'd been converted to internal combustion, bits had been added and she was in a poor state,' he recalls. Worn and disfigured, *Romp* was put away for six years before Percy was ready to begin the complete refurbishment she required.

A steam engine from a pinnace originally on HMS *Hood*, a boiler found in Napier, bits and pieces from a lifetime's trawling through auction rooms, a huge number of man hours — and there, in all her glory, is the *Romp* of today. Gleaming brass, immaculate paintwork, a tidy boiler, clean lines — it's easy to see why she is so admired by all who see her.

She's a film star too — *Romp* was chosen for her good looks for a TV series called 'Children of Fire Mountain'. She has steamed from Auckland to Ngunguru — no mean distance — following display at the Auckland Centenary Anniversary Regatta. For the technically minded, a Babcock Wilcox boiler feeds the AC Mumford engine, which drives the 20x33 three-bladed propellor, giving a speed of seven knots.

Romp's home is the Ngunguru River, and the setting, whether on the hard or alongside her berth, is near perfect. In the care he has lavished on her, the 15-year-old deck-boy in the Merchant Navy turned proud owner has breathed fresh life into the heritage of classic-boat builder Robert Logan and his talented team of over 100 years ago.

Rodger Girven

Rodger Girven glides alongside the wharf on the schooner *R Tucker Thompson*. Manoeuvring against the incoming tide, he berths her with an expertise honed by hundreds of hours at the controls. He's the skipper, and his knowledge and authority show.

'This is the perfect job. Where else could you do something you really love?'

There's a calm, easy-going manner about him as he snugs the boat down after a day charming the tourists on his Bay of Islands charter run. He finishes with a quick hose-down, then he's free for a beer and a yarn down below.

'I'm actually a painter and decorator. I started as a farmer but really I wanted something different. I began sailing about fifteen years ago and when this job came up I jumped at it.'

What does he do when he's not navigating *R Tucker Thompson* around the islands?

'I've got a mullety, actually — that's a story. A mate, Zeke Patterson, found the boat and restored her about twenty years ago. I bought the boat from him in her present condition. Most boats have a name, sail number, distinctive markings, but not this one. She's a phantom boat — no one knows anything about her.

'She's called *Gollum* — from *The Lord of the Rings*.'

A typical restoration story follows, but the basic construction was very sound.

'Carvel-built — double diagonal over,' Rodger explains. 'Zeke made the rig.'

Gollum draws 2 feet 11 inches, which is unusual for a mullety.

'I like the historical aspect of the mullet boats,' Rodger continues. 'They were classic working vessels. We race them now, but they were built as fishing boats. These guys would take off in the early morning, sail out to the fishing grounds, fish for as long as they could and then sail back to get the best price at the Auckland markets. Pushing the tide with just a light breeze on the nose, it must have taken forever to get home sometimes . . .'

He admits *Gollum* is hard to sail — 'She can be a real handful' — but the idea is to get her finished so he and his partner can do a bit of racing and cruising.

'There's an engine, but I don't think that's the way to go. I'd rather sail her.'

So Rodger sails for a living and intends to do the same for leisure as well.

'I didn't sail as a kid — I didn't come through that school. So to find myself doing it for both work and play is a bit different from what I expected.'

If you get the chance, take a cruise on *R Tucker Thompson*. The big, genial guy giving the orders is probably Rodger Girven. He's dying to talk to you about his mullet boat.

Sebastian Gundry

When your father has sailed round the world twice, you're likely to inherit a certain toughness and a calling for things nautical. Simon Gundry is a legend around the waterfront, so it's no wonder that his son Sebastian delights in the sea as well.

Sebastian's first efforts at boat building would not make prime exhibits at the Auckland Maritime Museum, but maybe they should. From an early age, Sebastian combed the foreshore and other areas of his Devonport hometown, on Auckland's North Shore, for scraps of polystyrene, plywood, cork and old bits of wood to build boats. Not models, you understand, but real boats that you sat in and sailed. Many a supermarket shopping bag was recycled to make sails.

The 14-year-old Rosmini College student is the second of five boys in his family, but he's always been a bit of a loner. Good at school and a leader in the Calliope Sea Scouts, he's turned out for his father's beloved North Shore Rugby Club, but he really prefers his own company. And boats have always been his main interest. After a day's sailing with his mates, when the others are all for heading home cold and wet, Sebastian always wants to go out again.

His dream has been to own a Hartley 16, one of the stalwarts of New Zealand yachting design. One day he found one at anchor in the upper reaches of Waitemata Harbour, much in need of TLC.

Perfect! But how to get it home, and how to pay for it? The first problem was easily solved, but not so the second.

It took a partnership with a friend and a hard-earned $800 from a paper round to secure ownership. But now the possibilities are endless, the horizon wide open and inviting exploration.

The Hartley is a frail craft, with no great capacity to venture far offshore. Nevertheless, it has taken Sebastian for an overnighter at Motutapu Island, and he has also spent nights in the lee of Brown's Island.

If Sebastian's father is concerned he doesn't show it, apart from insisting that Sebastian phone him at certain times during the trip. There is no parental pressure for Sebastian to follow in Dad's footsteps, just a quiet confidence in the young man's common sense and natural ability.

Sebastian's Hartley is named *Hippety Hop*, and it has already clocked up an impressive logbook of sea miles. It is a Saturday morning and, with Simon, I watch the fearsome threesome embark on yet another great adventure.

What next? There seems little doubt Sebastian will make the sea his domain. But for the time being it's a little wooden trailer sailer, a good mate and a thousand spots to visit and explore. Another round-the-world legend in the making? Watch this space.

John Hager

One of the many things New Zealand did for the American forces during the Second World War was build a fleet of 45-foot tugs for use around the Pacific theatre. The United Ship and Boat Building Company was set up for the purpose, the vessels being prefabricated at sites around Auckland and assembled in Freemans Bay. Fifty went into immediate service while a further 12 were ordered, but by the time these were built, the war was nearly over and they were sold off.

Matiu was one of them, and went to work for the Department of Agriculture, transporting everything from stock feed and building materials to the occasional VIP to and from the Somes Island quarantine station in Wellington Harbour. She performed these duties for 48 years, and also took part in the rescue of passengers from *Wahine*. She has always been a great sea boat; the only time in living memory that the weather stopped her was when 84-knot winds and 11-metre swells were recorded at Wellington Heads.

She came to the notice of John Hager, skipper of Auckland ferries and charter boats. John grew up sailing Ps around Point Chevalier and Westhaven in the 1950s before an agricultural science degree at Massey University took him out of yachting circulation. He returned to Auckland in the 1970s, where he resumed sailing with a Hartley trailer sailer and crewed on an M-class yacht. He picked up his skipper's ticket and worked on such well-known vessels as the *Te Aroha* and the Pride of Auckland fleet.

'I saw *Matiu* advertised for tender and couldn't resist the temptation,' says John, who has always had an affinity with historic wooden boats. 'But when my tender was successful, I found I owned a boat 580 nautical miles from where I wanted it to be.'

So *Matiu* returned home via East Cape, and at over 50 years old, is still at work.

'She's beautifully built of all the best materials,' explains John, thumping the solid keel. 'Imported Oregon pine, like all those tugs. I've kept her in survey, which allows me to take sightseers around the Hauraki Gulf. You'll see her most summers — we use her a lot.'

John has done his bit for the administration of recreational boating, and has served for eight years on the committee of one of Auckland's largest boating clubs, the Outboard Boating Club. He was commodore of the club for two years and was elected to life membership in 1998.

Matiu doesn't look quite the same as the vessel that slipped into Freemans Bay at the end of the war, but she's basically the same old tug that has done more than her fair share of service for her country.

Russell Harris

Russell Harris was digging post holes on his Dargaville farm one day.

'Suddenly,' he recalls, 'looking into one of those holes, a horrible thought struck me: "I'm going to be buried here."'

I'm sitting on the end of Opua Wharf in the Bay of Islands, and Russell is in full flight. His life story tumbles out at a relentless pace.

The change of direction at age 36. His first ocean trip, to Vanuatu. The trip to Thursday Island, where he was hired by the hospital as a carpenter and handyman. Hitching to Australia on a fishing boat. Crabbing at Weipa. Resumed acting and stage production with 'Annie Get Your Gun', then off into the sunset two months later, Phew! Slow down.

He did so by taking on the role of operations manager at Theatre Corporate in Auckland for one glorious year.

'Raymond Hawthorne — brilliant man. Got my vital juices flowing.'

But the wanderlust worked its charm once again and Russell found himself in Whangarei for the launch of the *Bounty* replica.

'Without any experience, I helped rig that ship. I just walked up and asked for a job.'

At about this time the remarkable story of the schooner *R Tucker Thompson* began. An American of that name had come to New Zealand with a young family. He began building a schooner in the tradi-

tional style, but unfortunately died. Over the next four years his son, Tod, carried on with the project, but it remained unfinished. Meanwhile, Russell had sold his Dargaville farm, and when asked by Tod to help fund the completion he declined. Then he had second thoughts.

'Maybe there was a place for creative, productive, traditional work in sailing, so I reconsidered,' says Russell, sighing deeply.

The partly constructed boat moved from Whangarei to the Harris section at Mangawhai Heads, but money worries, a shortage of skills, the passage of time and a general lack of resources conspired against the two workers. Undaunted, they forged on.

'Tod had the focus, I had the dream,' continues Russell.

Finally, after enough trials and tribulations to fill a book, *R Tucker Thompson* took to the water in all her painstakingly achieved glory. For the record, she is a copy of a Halibut topsail schooner — big, beamy, full-blooded.

'Each day she goes out with or without me, I can't help feeling I've got the greatest job in the world.'

This friendly, effusive man may just have found what we all strive for — the perfect lifestyle.

Maurice Hornsby

'I've never bought an aeroplane.' The significance of this statement soon becomes obvious as I chat with Maurice Hornsby in the comfortable living room of his Kerikeri home. 'I once had my photograph taken in front of a steam train. When my dad saw it, he said, "What the hell have you bought now?"'

It seems Maurice has a penchant for buying things — all sorts of things, houseboats included. 'Why a houseboat?' I enquire. 'Exactly,' sighs his wife, Leslie. 'There is a law in Fiji regarding proselytising,' explains Maurice. 'I thought, "Great, another law I can break." We intended selling Bibles from it, but that sort of fell over.' Clearly he is a man of great humour. He bought the houseboat from a guy in Whangarei, lived on it for a month and named it *Sam Hunt*. 'Rough around the edges, heart of gold.'

Space being short, let me summarise the life of *Sam Hunt*: towed from Whangarei to Auckland by yacht; nearly lost off Takatu, when the towline parted; arrived in Waitemata Harbour smack bang in the middle of a yacht race; moored in Westhaven Marina; clad in imitation bricks; a rotary clothesline erected on deck — not a good look; a pair of bloomers hoisted on aforementioned apparatus — an even worse look; authorities assumed people were living on board and asked them to leave.

'We've been on world TV. When the Pakistan World Cup cricket team was here, a news crew videoed them down at Westhaven and we were in the background. World famous we were!'

Maurice casually relates how the houseboat was sunk by a BMW. It seems that the car was left in neutral, took off, spilled off the wharf and was just saved by the mooring lines. The BMW was rescued, but the lines became caught under the wharf and when the next tide came in the houseboat was dragged under.

'We didn't know that until months afterwards, when an eyewitness came forward. Did I tell you we had a gin still on board? Plenty of power and water.' *Sam Hunt* has since gone from Westhaven. She's now moored at Waiheke, where she has a new owner.

But there were adventures with other vessels as well. 'I had *Eros*, a forty-five-foot Mummery. Took her out the first day I had her and ran straight into a bright-red container boat. The mast fell down — most embarrassing.' And adventures in business too. 'I had a second-hand/antique shop called Horrids of Parnell. Bought and sold all sorts of stuff. I stood outside Harrods in London handing out cards. I was hoping they would sue me!'

These days Maurice has a 40-foot Pelin launch. 'And a lot of other small boats around.' And cars. A real enthusiast, Maurice. The Rolls Royce Corniche in his garage has a huge wind-up key on the boot.

Wayne Larsen

When it comes to things mechanical, you either can or you can't. Understand them and fix them, that is. It's a whole new ball game when you can do both and build them as well.

Of all the mechanical devices designed and built to make boats move, the one that intrigues me most is the steam engine. I have never been able to figure out the principle of the thing — how the steam is regulated to a piston, which then turns a wheel, which is attached to a shaft, which is attached to the propeller. My eyes glaze over while the experts beam.

Wayne Larsen builds steam engines — ones that fizz and pump and make boats go.

'Stuart Turner is a well-known English manufacturer of steam engines,' he explains. 'I saw a lot of them and was sure I could build engines that worked just as efficiently but were less complicated and sold at a cheaper price.'

Steam has fascinated Wayne since his early days riding on the Devonport steam ferries and in his later years helping with the restoration and operation of the vintage steam tug, *William Daldy*. Today, Wayne works as a garage manager and is an automotive engineer by trade, so is around engines and machinery most of the time.

'I started to draw up a steam engine I thought would work. I built wooden patterns, then took them to the foundry to have them cast,' he continues.

Thus emerged the Mark 1 Larsen engine. It worked then, and still does.

'Where is it now?' I ask. 'In your boat?'

'As a matter of fact, it's in a guy's lounge.'

How do some blokes get away with that sort of thing?

Wayne then lapses into the jargon so beloved by steam freaks.

'I decided to buy a twin-simple instead of compounding.' Fellow steam-people, he assures me, will know exactly what he's on about.

More engines followed. Then, one day, he saw a hull — an old one — that he thought would be the perfect test-bed for his creations. So in went one of the latest, starting a long period of steam travel round the Hauraki Gulf. He tows the boat on a big trailer and often lights the boiler before he leaves home. He then literally steams down the highway, clouds billowing.

'It's practical to get the engine fired up, but it's also wonderful to see the looks on people's faces as we rush past.' He grins.

'Steam boats are an art form,' he continues. 'Engines and their polished brass come alive. When you light the fire, you bring something dead to life. It takes about four hundred hours to make one of these engines, and I hate to part with them. I think they should be stored in glass cases.'

Well, if someone's got one in their lounge, who knows? There could be others on display elsewhere. Steamies are truly a breed apart.

John Lidgard

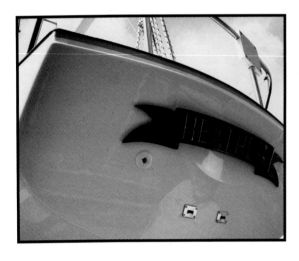

It's hard to know where to start with John Lidgard. The family name is famous, of course. The designer: his boats are everywhere. The builder: he's done as well as the best. His sons and grandchildren: they continue down the same road. There's a book to be written about the Lidgard contribution to boating in New Zealand, with half a dozen chapters reserved for John.

There was Fred (John's father), his uncle Roy and Mike: all were boat-builders. Roy was the boss of the Lidgard shipyard in the 1920s, when Arch Logan was still designing the odd boat. When John came on the scene, they were still building at Smelting House Bay on Kawau Island. 'Look at this,' he says, opening up a simple cash-book from the early business days. 'A complete boat for thirty-eight pounds — that's the lot. Here's one for seven pounds, twelve and sixpence. I don't think they made a lot of money.'

During his schooldays John loved the thrill of two-handed sailing with his mates. 'There used to be huge fleets at the Point Chev Boating Club in those days. Richmond, Ponsonby and Victoria were all at Westhaven — it was a great scene.' But he nursed a more ambitious desire: to go ocean racing. 'I read every book on the subject I could, by any author.' In 1956 he hopped on board his new yacht, *Matuku*, headed for Fiji and finished second. That was the start of a famous international career.

On the home front, in 1959 he built the first of a new class of boat called the Stewart 34, still highly competitive today. In 1960 he was on his own as a boat-builder. Since then, he's designed a lot of boats. 'About two hundred, I think.' Names that jog the memory: *Regardless*, *Reward*, *Runaway*. 'In 1971, New Zealand finished first, second and third in the Southern Cross Cup in Australia, winning the ultimate prize: the Sydney–Hobart. Brin Wilson was first. I was second. Chris Bouzaid was third. That will never be done again.'

From the John Lidgard fact file: 230,000 ocean miles; 21 crossings of the Tasman; still called on to ferry boats around the world and occasionally to race; still designing boats — he's drawing one up as I talk to him.

John's children and grandchildren make him beam with delight. 'My son Duthie has a boat-building yard just a stone's throw from here. My grandsons sail — young Tim has come on delivery voyages with me.' Today John's son Duthie owns *Heather*, a boat John built in 1945, when he was eighteen.

His biggest moment? No hesitation. '1981 around the North Island two-handed. Heather and I beat my eldest son, Kevin, by twelve hours, and he had a bigger boat.' He rubs his hands, the memory still sweet.

The Lidgards have given yachting in this country plenty. I'm sure it's given them plenty in return.

Jim Lowe

'**I look** after her, she looks after me.'

The comment comes from Jim Lowe on a crisp Napier morning. The sun is shining and the water glassy as we glide towards *Chinchilla*, Jim's Stewart 42, swinging on the piles in Napier's yacht anchorage.

'Only five were built,' Jim explains. 'They were designed to be Gulf racers, and this one was a spec boat built by Max Carter.

'I've got salt water in my veins. 'You could say it infected me but inoculated my brother.'

Jim is *Chinchilla*'s third owner. He bought her in 1990, and according to his logs and own reckoning has clocked up some 60,000 sea miles, mostly as a solo sailor.

'You either like single-handed or you don't — there's no halfway. I like it, and during all the years I've been sailing I've never had a close call. The over-riding fear of a solo sailor is to be run down by a container ship while asleep at night. I've never had a close shave — not that I know of, anyway.'

Jim is a diver by trade, doing the hard yards on the hydro schemes around New Zealand. It was as a ten-year-old that he began his lifelong relationship with the sea. His folks had built a ketch in Havelock North, and a four-year Pacific cruise fuelled the youngster's desire to spend more time on the ocean.

'*Chinchilla* is so easy to sail — my best twenty-four hours solo is two hundred and three miles, which is outstanding.'

I notice a small kiwi emblem painted on the self-steering.

'I was in Turkey,' explains Jim. 'There was absolutely nothing to remind me of home, so I printed the little bird to help me remember where I came from and was heading to.'

Anchoring on his own in strange places holds little fear for Jim.

'Although I have been known to hot-wire the boat with a few thousand volts. Watch out anyone touching the handrails.'

What next for Jim?

'I might have another go at the New Plymouth to Mooloolaba, but I've got a family now and want to involve them.'

Remarkably enough, they haven't been put off ocean cruising, despite taking seventeen hours to get from Cape Palliser to Tory Channel in a foul Cook Strait — a journey that should take only a fraction of that time.

I've never understood why people would want to sail solo on extended voyages. Jim Lowe has done it dozens of times, so if you want to know, perhaps you'd better ask him.

Mike Maffey

Is the person to be found who, by look or deed, typifies the famous New Zealand boatie? Does the 'average bloke', so lovingly invoked by a former prime minister, really exist? Relaxing over a cold beer on a hot day, I think I've found a guy who fits all of the above. I'm in the Hibiscus Coast Boating Club sitting opposite Mike Maffey.

'I was climbing around in boats before I could walk,' confides Mike. 'I've owned boats since I was eleven.'

I'm reminded of Roy Dickson and others as he describes how the kids in those days used to scrape tar off the roads to keep their corrugated iron punts afloat. Cherubs, Ps, Qs and Zephyrs came and went before the first keel boat at age 20. This was soon followed by a 30-foot John Spencer-designed Sabre.

I know I'm getting close to the heartland of New Zealand boating with Mike's next remark: '*Excalibur* had an engine that didn't work, so we threw it out. Made more room for the beer!'

In the wake of this legendary example of floating Kiwi ingenuity came *Samarkand*, a 34-footer, but the big blow of 1975 ripped her from her Okahu Bay mooring and splintered her on the rocks.

From here the CV begins to build.

'I ran charter boats in the Bay of Islands. Tried game fishing as well, but I wasn't too good at that.'

Then Mike headed for New Guinea, where he ran a game boat when he wasn't driving a tug. He

grins. 'It was a great life, trading fish, prawns, deer and pigs. Marvellous.'

Then came a sharp reminder of mortality. A heart attack cut him down, and he knew it was time to return home. But Mike continued his colourful career aboard other people's launches, running their operations for them. Now he works out of Gulf Harbour with a 31-foot displacement launch, which he uses for regular trips to the Barrier and Coromandel.

About six years ago, a friend, John Flyger, persuaded Mike to come down to the local boat club. Thus began an association that today is as staunch as they come.

'Some of my exploits might sound a bit irresponsible,' Mike confesses. Some not printed here do, but dedication to safe boating is now one of his primary concerns. The club has recently put a new rescue boat on the water, a project of which Mike has been a part. He also takes rescue and boatmaster courses — he currently has 30 people under tuition. And this most active of boat clubs runs a fishing contest on the first Sunday of every month.

So what have we got? A fishing, tutoring boatie with a mountain of memories and a stack of stories. A bloke who's spent a lifetime at sea. In short, an archetypal Kiwi joker.

I think Mike Maffey would be happy with that description.

Kim McDell

Kim McDell grew up in Waipu, where you went sailing in a footy jersey and bare feet. Son of the legendary 'Pop' McDell, who would go on to become Commodore of the Royal New Zealand Yacht Squadron, Kim, in company with his brother Terry, was destined to become a world force in the spectacular 18-foot class. But the seven-year-old had to learn the ropes fast and early.

'Pop put me up forward in his X-class, *Davina*. There I was with my kapok life jacket going over the Waipu bar. I can still see that.

'Pop ran several businesses in Waipu, but his passion was 18-footers. Each Sunday in summer we would leave at five a.m. to drive to Auckland, race the boat, inevitably capsize and spend two or three hours in the water. It was impossible to get upright. Eventually we'd get to shore, dry off (sort of) and drive back to Waipu. Nobody had heard of hypothermia in those days.'

It would be fair to say the McDell boys had 18-footers drilled into them.

'There were fifteen or sixteen boats then. The adrenaline rush of an eighteen-footer at full speed, with others in a race right beside you, is unbelievable.'

Moving to King's College in Auckland introduced Kim to a new challenge: athletics. He was good enough to break the New Zealand junior 880 yards record and the junior mile record.

'I ran against Peter Snell, too,' he drops in, before returning to the theme of sailing. 'Pop bought the K-class keeler, *Waiomo*. We raced her as a family.'

But the lure of the 18s was strong. In 1970 Terry was racing on Tom Clark's *Buccaneer* overseas, but when Travelodge stepped in with 18-footer sponsorship, he returned home to accompany Kim to Brisbane for the world championships.

'We didn't win,' recalls Kim, 'but we sure knew we were on the right track.' The 1974 championships were scheduled for Auckland, and with Terry steering and Kim and Peter Brooke crewing, the coveted world title came home to Waipu. 'Great moment, great series.' Kim beams. He garnered another world title with Peter Wilcox and Peter Walker in the half-ton *Gunboat Rangiriri*.

Kim and Bruce Farr have always had a strong relationship. Kim, in the boat-building business for 25 years, acknowledges, 'We've built about a thousand boats to Bruce's designs.'

These days, Kim is in partnership in the McDell-built Farr 41 MX *Zamzamah*. His lifestyle now centres on the business, but he will never forget the glory days of the 18s — he gets goosebumps just thinking about it.

Two world sailing titles and New Zealand athletic records — those alone look pretty good on the CV.

Jim McGlashan

Aramoana **has** the classic lines and so she should. The concept was the great Arch Logan's, and Bill Couldrey built her. She came with a crop of Auckland racers in 1938, including *Matatua Ghost* and — arguably the most famous of all — Lou Tercel's *Ranger*. It was a vintage year.

Aramoana was built for Gordon Pollard of the Manakau Timber Company, and can count among her few owners Battle of Britain hero Sir Keith Park.

Jim's journey to *Aramoana* followed the route many classic-yacht owners have travelled. The Captain Hornblower books delivered an early inspirational message, then it was on to Outward Bound.

'My first boat was a Hartley day-sailer. We did trips out of Whakatane.' Then came a Windrush 14 catamaran, which he raced out of the Whakatane Yacht Club.

In 1983 Jim settled on an orchard in Kerikeri and was determined to own a boat.

'Got a little Robert Tucker twenty-three-footer. I think we did about twelve hundred miles that year just in and around the bay.' But Jim needed something bigger, so bought the 39-foot cutter *Aramoana*.

The top of the mast broke off shortly after purchase, so a painted aluminium replacement was fitted.

'I made quite a few sets of oars from that mast. But there was an interesting thing — when I split the mast, inside I found the signatures of *Aramoana*'s owners during the mid 1950s.'

The owner before Jim had put in an engine, built a dog house on top and rewired the whole boat.

'I had to get rid of Sir Keith Park's toilet — it was pretty unreliable.'

In 1988 *Aramoana* came out of the water for 18 months while Jim painstakingly burnt her back to the original wood and generally brought her back up to scratch. The interior was totally stripped out and rebuilt in modern traditional style. The refit was made easier by a set of line drawings, which Jim discovered in a 1953 edition of *Sea Spray*. In her current configuration the boat comfortably sleeps six, as long as they are friends. 'She's easily driven, too — I've towed her for miles with the dinghy when there's been no wind.'

Jim is owner/operator of the Opua Floating Dock, but is ready for a new challenge.

'That won't affect *Aramoana*. I'm smartening her up for the classic-yacht regatta, and have given her her first set of new sails in thirty years.'

Jim concludes with a few general thoughts on boating in the Bay of Islands.

'It's great being in a bay all by yourself. One gourmet meal after another. I'll never be without a boat.'

Bill Couldrey died in 1998 and another irreplaceable part of New Zealand yachting history went with him. But craft like *Aramoana* sail on, making sure his great contribution will be remembered.

Ngaio McMillan

As the television commercial for Mainland Cheese says: 'Good things take time.'

The 52-foot yacht in Ngaio McMillan's weather-beaten shed in Epuni, in the heart of Lower Hutt, has had a gestation longer than most. Ngaio completed the plans in 1980, but he'd begun thinking his dream through 20 years earlier. As the boat is still a little way from seeing the water, the whole venture will probably amount to 30 years.

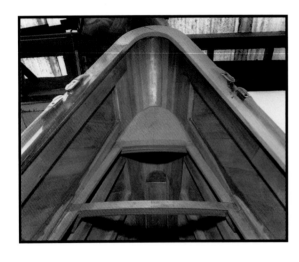

'We've always been as mad as maggots about boats,' says a beaming Ngaio in a down-to-earth sort of way. 'Dad was keen on the Marlborough Sounds so we went to live there in 1933. I'm one of seven kids, and we've always loved the sea.'

In his time Ngaio has been a professional photographer, but his skill in boat design and construction comes from his years as an engineer. 'I spent sixteen years with Southwards; most of this area was pegged out by me when they were putting in the new power supplies.'

The attention to detail required when formulating complex designs has helped him develop a combination of conceptual thinking and practical ability.

What Ngaio is attempting to create is a high-performance sailing houseboat, and looking at this yacht taking up every square inch of his back-yard shed it is obvious he has nearly succeeded. Almost every feature has been thought through and adapted for maximum efficiency — things you wouldn't notice if he didn't point them out, such as how the bunks work in conjunction with the storage lockers, or how the companionways lead logically to the service areas. And everything has the McMillan twist to it. Take the stern, where his extraordinary ideas have found expression in a variety of unique design features.

All up she weighs 14 tons, will draw 7 feet and she's built mainly of kauri and redwood, so she's a solid Cook Strait boat if ever there was one.

There are two questions that I just have to ask.

'How will you get it out? It's in a shed behind your house.'

'No problem,' says Ngaio, with faultless engineering logic. 'I've bought the house next door and there's room to fit a crane down the side there.'

I'm impressed. Nevertheless . . .

'It's been a while, Ngaio.' I don't want to say it. 'Will it see the water?'

The hearty chuckle this elicits is a characteristic McMillan prelude to an emphatic answer.

'Of course. I haven't come this far to be lumbered with a museum piece. She'll sail all right, and she'll be a beauty.'

This bloke knows his boat well. I await launch day.

Ray Morris

The fact that Ray Morris sailed 4000 miles from Panama to the Marquesas without charts, referring only to a 1940s atlas his wife happened to have brought along, says a fair bit about his innate sailing skill — and perhaps more than a little about Ray the man.

'I actually drew a chart from the atlas,' he explains, 'which worked.'

Ray's life story has all the twists and turns of a good novel. Devonport-born, he would have been unusual not to be into boating. 'I just loved yachts. I quite often didn't make it to school. When I left to work at the post office, I quite often didn't make it there either.'

He decided to head off to England, working in nuclear power stations and surveying oil tankers.

'I bought a boat and met a lady — in that order. The lady and I married, and I asked her if she wanted to sail to New Zealand. She said yes.'

But the boat wasn't right for the job, so he sold it and built a steel one. And so it was they made it to the Marquesas.

'But there we had a big build-up of barnacles on the bottom. The only way to get them off was to dive, but there were hundreds of sharks swimming around. The locals told me to get in the water between ten a.m. and two p.m., as the sharks didn't feed at that time of day. I did, and they didn't. Lucky, I guess.'

Then it was on to Fiji, where the two of them were promptly thrown in jail. 'Muldoon had clamped down on overstayers in New Zealand, and we were charged with the same crime in retaliation. The judge threw the case out in about five minutes and we made it to New Zealand.' But they didn't stay long.

'I wanted to sail back to England, so off we went again.' They hadn't got further than Devonport Wharf before the boat caught fire.

'Not a great omen, eh?'

The log shows it took them 53 days to get to Cape Horn, 71 days to Montevideo, and another 91 days to Falmouth. What it doesn't record, however, is that Ray's wife disembarked on arrival and hasn't sailed with him since.

'I sold the boat to another lunatic and came back to New Zealand.'

Ray sailed a Noelex 22 for a while but now owns a Farr 30-footer — *Blaze Away*.

'I take off early morning, pop up to Tutukaka, have a pie, hop across to Coromandel, have another pie, and come home again.'

His worst moment ever?

'Being knocked overboard in the South Atlantic. I just managed to grab the rail as it rushed past. I still sweat when I think about it.'

If you spot a weather-beaten sea dog wrapping a smile round a pie in Tutukaka or Coromandel, chances are you're looking at Ray Morris.

Rob Morton

I once read that the New Zealand dream is to own a place on an island, have a boat, do some cruising and fishing, maybe a little work, and then rest.

Rob Morton might not be flattered to hear his existence described in these terms, but on nearly all counts his lifestyle and the dream list match.

Consider: he lives on Waiheke Island; he has a boat, of which more shortly; he cruises (a little); he races (a bit); I'm sure he catches the odd fish; and he propagates trees for a living. OK — with so much going on, maybe he doesn't have time to rest.

Castor Bay used to be alive with a hundred centreboard dinghies on Sunday mornings. Rob began in a P-class and as he grew he progressed to Moths, Cherubs and Zeddies. Then it was onward and upward, all the way to square riggers. Distant lands beckoned — England, sub-Antarctica, Moruroa. Rob has travelled many adventurous miles. Then in 1989 he met Hanne and they settled on Waiheke.

'I used to have a boat called *Dodo*. She's now a little steamboat called *Zeltic*. Not a great sailboat, *Dodo*. I once took twenty-three hours to get from Great Barrier to Kawau on my own, so I thought something a little better on the wind would be kinder.'

Rob's brother-in-law did the drawings, down came some Waiheke macrocarpas, the lengths were milled at Ostend, and *Paketi* began to take shape. Twenty-four feet long and eight feet wide, she slipped into the tide in 1992. 'Nearly everything is hand-made. I've never spent much time in chandleries.'

Sails were laid out and stitched in the local hall, spars fashioned by hand, and the fittings mostly home-made. *Paketi* harks back to the era of scows and luggers, those work-horses of a thousand water-ways, and she earns her living as well.

You couldn't count the number of trees she's carted around the Hauraki Gulf. With his propagation business, Rob sells a wide variety of both natives and exotics. And *Paketi* gets them to their destinations. Walk past some recently planted trees on Auckland's North Shore, and chances are they're Rob Morton saplings.

Rob has crammed as many as 1700 newly sprouted trees on board. Compost, timber for milling, a tow horse for macrocarpa logs — *Paketi* has carried them all. She's raced as well, cleaning up her division of the Mahurangi Regatta three times.

'Ralph Sewell once said, "*Paketi* sails like a hairy goat." I think that was a compliment . . .'

He's slow getting the boat out of winter mode this season. Why? Some swallows have nested under the tarpaulin cover.

'I don't have the heart to boot them out. I'll let nature do her thing before I get back on the water.'

Perhaps there'll be time for a little rest after all.

Tom Partridge

'I love skippering this little boat. She weighs around two-and-a-half tons — a little different from my last ship, which was around forty-two thousand tons.'

Pardon?

Tom Partridge nudges the little Bruce Askew-designed day boat into its privileged berth in Kerikeri. The 42,000 tonner he refers to was his command in the merchant navy, the international container vessel *New Zealand Pacific*. The two-and-a-half tonner is *Aldeburgh Gypsy*, his delightful little run-around in the Bay of Islands.

'*Aldeburgh Gypsy* is the boat that built itself,' he continues. An explanation is clearly called for, so he goes back to the beginning.

Tom is the great grandson of a cod banger — a self-explanatory title. Born in Felixstowe, he grew up in Brightlingsea surrounded by wartime seacraft — torpedo boats, minesweepers — and countless fishing boats. At nautical college in Southampton he began in earnest what was to become a lifelong acquaintance with the sea. He emigrated to New Zealand, married a Kiwi lass and went on to work for both the New Zealand Shipping Corporation and the Pacific Forum Line before retiring to Kerikeri.

Always good with his hands, Tom admired the lines of the Askew boat in a magazine and decided it was for him. He stumbled on a heap of not-too-bad kauri — very hard to obtain — and bought a stack. This raw material, plus his boat-building skills, plus the Askew design — and hey presto. There she was, the little 22-footer that is the *Aldeburgh Gypsy*. The name comes from the fishing smack Tom's great grandfather operated out of Aldeburgh.

'She's a little less stressful to put into a berth than a container ship,' he confides, betraying a weakness for understatement.

These days Tom takes off for a leisurely two or three days' fishing every week, with his wife or one of his mates, around New Zealand's paradise islands. The great-grandson of a Aldeburgh cod banger has come a long way.

Rhys Pearson

There's no getting away from it. Jesus' instruction to Peter when he was having little luck fishing on the Sea of Galilee, 'Try casting your net on the other side', repeatedly comes to mind as I listen to Rhys relate his numerous fishing exploits.

Rhys is a Presbyterian minister and not given to telling fishy tales, but to hear how he has fished from both sides of his boat — and done very well thank you — is enough to make any other fisherman envious. There's no getting away from it — he's had to have had divine intervention on his side.

Rhys has been visiting the same camping spot on the Coromandel Peninsula for nearly 20 years now, and although the days of logging each catch are long gone, he has his memories — which, if his current exploits are anything to go by, are perfectly reliable.

So what sort of boat contributes to these catches of just about everything you could imagine, from crayfish to snapper, John Dory to kahawai — you name it? A 26-foot killer-craft with enormous outboards searching miles out to sea? Nah! A nine-foot dinghy with a five-horsepower motor. Seriously.

You have to see it to believe it: two, sometimes three, people in a boat that looks not much bigger than an upturned wheelie bin in seas in which the Ancient Mariner would have cried foul.

But Rhys is nothing if not careful. 'If you saw some of the weather we venture out in, you'd know why we always wear lifejackets,' he says.

A little blue sailing dinghy is the current model, and has been since 1979, but Rhys began boat-building long before then. A canoe made of calico was an early effort. 'Five coats of paint inside and seven outside,' he relates. 'The whole thing was held together with paint.'

Other vessels and adventures followed: 'Racing in a Zeddie had its moments, like when we put the mast through the bottom. That tended to slow it down.'

After a marine-materials familiarisation course at Hamilton Polytechnic (not a boat-building course, mind), work on the blue beauty began, based on a set of Jim Young plans. All Rhys's children have seen the sea from this boat, pottering around the rocks near the beach at Waikawau Bay. In 20 years of fishing, she has brought literally tonnes of fish to shore — a classic case of bigger not necessarily being better.

But what about, one day, another boat? A new boat? A larger boat?

'Don't know,' says Rhys. 'Maybe when I retire. This year at Waikawau I might just try casting on the other side. It worked for Peter. I'm pretty sure it'll work for me.'

Hugh Poole

As a bit of romantic I like stories with happy endings.

The story of Hugh Poole and his 14-foot X-class *Charade* is a tale of triumph, loss, pursuit and, finally, jubilant reunification — with all the makings of a classic Hollywood screenplay. It's a spin on the age-old formula: bloke meets boat, bloke does well with boat, bloke loses boat, bloke tries to get boat back, bloke finally prevails.

First, the bloke.

Hugh Poole has achieved much in a lifetime of sailing. The Heretaunga Boating Club at Petone has a long and proud tradition in Wellington yachting, and young Hugh eased his first mainsail on a P-class there in 1939.

National success in 1956 with the Moffat Cup in the Idle-along class led to a second place in 1958 in the X-class Sanders Cup, followed by retirement at the ripe old age of 34 — for about two minutes. Poole came roaring out of his armchair to crew with Pat Millar in *Valiant* and take the coveted Sanders Cup in 1960. It is now a matter of record that Hugh Poole, with crew Tony Dobbs and Graeme Morris in *Charade*, won the Sanders Cup four times in a row — 1967 to 1970 inclusive — a feat achieved by no one before or since.

The innovations of mast and sail contributed hugely to that success on the boat they called *Charade*. She was, and is, a superyacht.

'The Poole rocketship,' Hugh recalls, grinning broadly. 'Well ahead of her time — a great boat.'

But *Charade*'s day came and went. In 1971 the Javelin replaced the X-class as the Sanders Cup yacht and Hugh decided to sell her, a decision he later regretted. 'I sold my engineering business in 1992 and embarked on a quest to find her again. I advertised everywhere for two years, without success.'

Then, by sheer chance, Christchurch yachtsman Graham Mander saw an X-class advertised in a local publication, took a look at her and concluded that those lines, and those beautifully engineered home-made fittings, could only belong to *Charade*.

Hugh Poole rescued the now bright-orange masterpiece and began a full restoration, almost 30 years to the day since she was launched. Jack Cropp, who moulded the hull, would be truly proud of how she looks today — once more in her original state, with gleaming mahogany, immaculate paintwork, and the original, highly innovative fittings.

Hugh Poole — Wellington's most distinguished yachtsman, team manager at two Olympic Games, Soling representative at the Montreal Olympics in 1976 — has one final role in mind for *Charade*.

'I want this boat to be displayed. She's a vital part of New Zealand's yachting history. A museum would be a fitting place for her.' I'll drink to that.

Bloke loses boat, bloke finds boat. Don't you just love it when a romance works out?

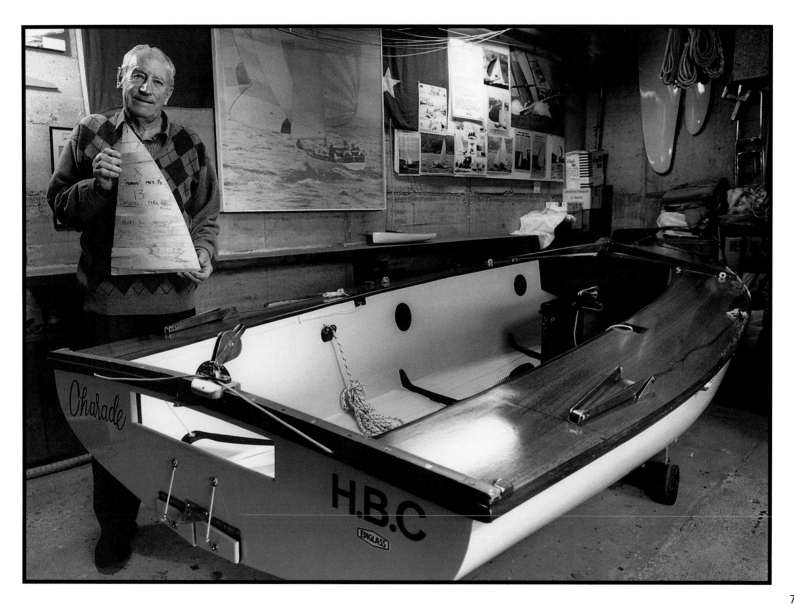

Mick Reynolds

Tern II - now there's a nice play on words.

Perched high on the hard stand by the Weiti Boating Club at Whangaparaoa, the English-built wooden yacht looks in need of some TLC. And that's just what Mick Reynolds is administering. He's knocking the boat into shape for a world cruise to raise popular consciousness about family violence.

'Anyone who has lost a family member to violence by another can have their name on the sail.'

The idea belongs to an American, Lyn Avatar, and so does the boat. She bought it from Mike a couple of years ago.

'It's my job to get her ready, though,' he explains.

Now this is an interesting vessel. From the Lloyds register of 1899:

> *Wooden yacht*
> *Construction: Heart oak pitch pipe*
> *Topsides: Teak*
> *Built by: Stow and Son, Southampton*

Claud Worth, who owned her around 1910, wrote in his book *Classic Cruising*: '*Tern II* is a fast boat — best to windward in a fresh breeze, light to steer and steady. One has the impression of orderly and irresistible advance, such as I have never experienced.' Praise indeed.

Tern II was present in 1939 when the British Expeditionary Force was hauled off the beaches of Dunkirk. She was damaged, but only a little.

In 1952 she sailed to New Zealand, and spent the next 20 years in Thames. When Mick was looking round for a catamaran to sail in the Pacific, his mate Bill Cunningham suggested he look her over.

'She was up to her bunks in mud, looking awful . . . While we were cleaning the cabin we happened upon an old green bottle with a rusty lid. Off came the top and we drank the best hundred-year-old Scotch you can imagine.' He ducks below, and returns proudly brandishing the bottle.

Thus did Mick become the proud owner of his first sailing boat.

Mick's family strain tends more towards the Welsh, as reflected by his choice of background music. His mother was Irish.

'I've been forty years in the defence forces here and in Britain. At the moment I'm an air-traffic controller at Whenuapai.'

Mick's spare time is taken up with getting *Tern II* shipshape for the big trip. She is due to leave for Hawaii in May, and he wants to join her in Britain.

'There's still quite a lot to do though — I haven't put a motor in yet. I've bought a depth sounder but don't have the heart to drill another hole in her.'

All things going well, *Tern II* will once again set her sails and embark on another mission not dissimilar to that which took her to Dunkirk — rescuing people from the violence of the world.

Pete Richards

'When I first saw her, I said to myself, "She's absolutely gorgeous."'

The speaker is Pete Richards; the object of his affection, *Undine*.

Now here's a grand old piece of history. Built in 1895, *Undine* was originally a Fullers boat built to carry kauri gum, operating in and around the Kerikeri inlet. She was a 35-foot centreboarder with a broad 9 foot, 6 inch beam, ideal for the shallow coastal waters she was designed for. In those days she had an open cockpit and a high peak gaff rig.

In her early days *Undine* did service around the Cape Brett lighthouse, the Thames goldfields and along the northern coast. She ended up on the beach at Mangawhai, and Ralph Sewell, the builder of *Breeze* and owner of *Ripple* (see page 82), undertook her first restoration. Later Alan Brimblecombe, who began *Undine*'s restoration as a steamboat, bought her. *Undine* subsequently spent at lot of time in Auckland, where she was owned by Bruce Marler, former Commodore of the Royal New Zealand Yacht Squadron, and John Duder.

So how did Pete and *Undine* meet?

The boat was put up for sale and advertised in various publications. Pete spotted one of the ads and decided a first-hand inspection was in order. What followed can only be described as love at first sight. But, like many love affairs, the road was rocky at first for Pete and *Undine*. Quite simply, he couldn't afford to tie the knot. He'd been a teacher for many years, including a five-year stint in the Bahamas. When he came home, he decided on a complete change of direction and completed a certificate of maritime tourism at Northland Polytechnic, before tutoring on the very same course. It was quite a while before the boat became his, and he candidly admits he'll be paying her off for some time to come.

'She was licensed to carry thirty passengers in 1900. I'm putting her back into survey so at least she can earn some of her keep. There are no winches on board, and I'm reluctant to put in a forward bulkhead.'

He goes on to sum up the preoccupation so many blokes have with old beauties of the sea like *Undine*.

'You take her out in a dying breeze, when the sun's setting and the tide's against you — and time just stands still. She creaks and groans — you have to slow down. You can't rush her. You know you're really sailing. I want to sail her in a classic race in 2000 — that will be her third century under sail.'

Of course, the work on a vessel of *Undine*'s vintage is never-ending, and at present she's on the hard, still being coaxed back to complete fitness. But when she's made it, she'll have another lifetime of sailing before her.

Undine — one hundred and thirteen years young.

Harold Saunders

There can be few more inspiring sights in New Zealand than the outer Tory Channel, in the Marlborough Sounds, early on a crisp winter's morning with the sun just up, no breeze, a flat sea and those towering headlands. Isolated, but idyllic.

We race into the bay at about 9.30 on just such a morning, the temperature hovering around five degrees. Harold Saunders greets me in his boat shed with a warm handshake and a mile-wide Mainlander smile. There are four boats there: one, his own, all but finished; another, for a local publican, almost there; and two others, a way to go and buyers yet to be found.

'Not a lot of call for this type of boat these days. There aren't many of us working with wood now.'

What a shame. These works of art have to be seen to be believed. This sort of workmanship has come from a time well past. In fact, Harold learnt his trade from his father. The Saunders were once world famous in Paremata, north of Wellington.

'Sailing P-class, dinghy racing, rugby on the beach, swimming every day — I had a great upbringing,' he says. 'My father was tough, though. If you deserved a boot in the backside, you got one.'

Regional bylaw bureaucracy, relating to the marine business, eventually forced the Saunders out and they moved to the more hospitable Sounds, to the property on Arapawa Island, accessible only by boat.

Harold has lived here for 34 years.

History is all around. Jackson's Bay is named after the Jackson settlers of the early 19th century, and sitting in the front room of Harold's house you can see James Jackson's well-kept grave 30 metres away, on a small hill. The famous whaling Peranos bought the property from the Jacksons, and Harold bought 1000 acres from Joe Perano in 1966. He's shifted across the property and built sheds and houses, but the key to his life here is boat-building. It is with pride that he shows me the half-models in his workroom. He picks one up with great care.

'This one was wrecked,' he sighs. 'Great boat. Took me a year and they put it on the bloody rocks.'

Piles of diagrams, photographs and the models testify to a lifetime of hard work and achievement. Wooden boats from Harold Saunders might cost a bit more than your average vessel, but oh, the attention to detail, the craftsmanship — and all done without a general store in sight.

'I've got to get it right with what I have. Can't just step out and get some new parts or equipment.

'Maybe we've spent enough time here,' he muses. 'Maybe it's time to move into town.'

No more Saunders boats then? Who knows? But one thing's for sure: there are two partly constructed beauties in the shed just waiting for owners. To be finished to your own design and specification.

Why not give him a bell?

Ralph Sewell

These days Ralph Sewell doesn't swing onto his 40-footer, *Ripple*, in quite the way he used to. After all, he's 78, and a stroke a few years ago that robbed him of the use of one arm has all but ended his active boating. 'I'm almost a single-handed sailor these days,' he reminds me two or three times during our conversation. Clearly each task he takes on is now that little bit harder than before.

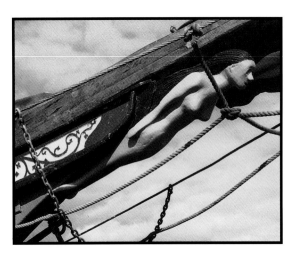

It's a perfect day as we step into Ralph's dinghy — one of hundreds he's built — to take a closer look at *Ripple*, rocking gently on an ebb tide in the centre of the bay. *Ripple* is a 25-year-old replica cutter. On deck we can see an untidy tangle of ropes, and the bolts have given in to the sea.

Built of Californian redwood in just nine months, without any plans, by a guy who hated school and had no formal boat-building or engineering training, it's a pretty impressive achievement. Cutters like this were common at the turn of the century, carting everything from livestock to gravel and timber all round the northern coastline. This one plied the waters from Houhora to the Mercury Islands. Ralph even used *Ripple* to shift house.

The cramped saloon is clearly well lived in, but the coal range seems a bit out of place. Hanging right next to it is a wood carving fashioned by Ralph's wife, Alison, who died some years ago. Kerosene lamps sway from various hooks at forehead-knocking height, and pervading everything is the musty smell of diesel mixed with salt, coal dust and sea air. Rumpled bunks, chipped coffee cups, tins of this and that — this is no boat-show centrepiece.

Ralph came to New Zealand as a four-year-old from Nottinghamshire. On leaving school he made a living as a young apprentice in Devonport, building wooden dinghies. This was the start of a lifetime's work, involving a variety of jobs but all related to his passion — the sea.

Ralph was hit by Rob Muldoon's boat tax in the 1980s, which he defied. A long battle ensued, and he narrowly escaped going to jail. He recalls the incident with some amusement, but you can still glimpse the underlying resentment. He saw many boat-builders — some of them good friends — go to the wall at that time.

In later years Ralph built the brigantine *Breeze*, now in the Auckland Maritime Museum. Again he used no plans; it was simply a case of a great eye coupled with a natural talent. Ralph's legacy lives on not only in *Ripple* and *Breeze* but also in a host of other boats still in commission around the coast.

'If it looks good from any angle, it's a good boat,' says Ralph. Take a look at *Ripple* or *Breeze* and see if he's right.

*Ralph Sewell died on Christmas Day 1999, having sailed *Ripple* from Waiheke Island to Clevedon the day before to spend Christmas with his family.

Dennis Shepherd

Dennis Shepherd is a Hamilton physiotherapist who has been in and around boats for most of his life. From the classic Kiwi-kid syndrome of Moths and Cherubs to Farr 3.7s, 14-foot skiffs and a national title — the path of a typical New Zealand boating bloke.

The son of a Methodist minister, Dennis began sailing at the age of eleven. His father had learnt to sail as a missionary in the Solomon Islands and was keen to teach his son the basics.

'I had a sailfish, which is the equivalent of a surfboard with a sail on it,' he explains.

This was a guy who, from those early days, was clear about his ambitions and had a planned timeframe in which to achieve his yachting goals.

'I remember the 1972 World Cherub Championships well. I was the only competitor with a wooden mast. I mowed six lawns a week to pay for my first new sail.'

In Auckland pursuing his physiotherapy qualification, Dennis couldn't afford a boat. Eventually, as his situation improved, he got into a Farr 3.7. Among Dennis's goals was winning a national yachting championship within six years — and that's what he did. He held the 3.7 title for four years, from 1984 to 1988.

Back in Hamilton with his own physiotherapy practice going, he decided to expand the class.

'As class secretary I bought a mould from High Modulus and was convinced by an Australian boat-builder that between us we could turn out a boat a week.'

The trouble was, the first one took 12 weeks to complete. 'I had to work the practice during the day and try to keep up with the boats at night.'

The fleet grew from four to 24 in Hamilton. Dennis fondly recalls that there were 48 boats at the national championships.

A two-year break from sailing followed, then he was right back into it in one of the most sensational of all classes — the 14-foot skiff, 'an animal of a boat at the best of times'. In 1997 he won the New Zealand Championships and went to the world championships in San Francisco as the team physiotherapist and sailor.

'Ironically it was me who was injured — major carpal-tunnel problems in both hands. We were second equal with the Australians in the team racing, but I was unable to complete the main competition. I sold the boat there and came home for surgery.'

But Dennis is sailing 14s again, after a new boat-building venture, when he isn't working in his practice or being a physio for the Chiefs and the Waikato NPC rugby team.

'We all have to work to pay for the sailing habit,' he comments. How true.

Barry Simmonds

As a youngster Barry Simmonds did what so many New Zealand kids do — built model boats from any and all available bits and pieces and sailed them. Holidaying at his grandparents' home in Herne Bay, Auckland, put him at the water's edge, which gave him plenty of opportunity.

'Since then the number and variety of boats owned by myself and my three sons is incredible,' says Barry.

Maybe his favourite is the mullety, *Tao Tane*.

'My sons and I had three mulleties at one stage. That was eighteen guys on the water as crew every Saturday. Gun of the day was eighty-year-old Vic Lidgard — what a sailor!'

It was the custom then to ballot for a boat to sail from Point Chevalier to the Ponsonby Cruising Club. Barry drew *Tao Tane*, raced her and won.

'I fell in love with her there and then,' he confesses. 'I beat Vic so I had to have her.'

And, in 1973, have her he did. Of all the new fibreglass mullet boats, Barry found *Honey* — originally owned by Jim Davern — the most elusive. In 1981 Barry rerigged *Tao Tane* in her original gaff configuration, and in 1983 she was club champion, but in 1986 she was sold due to illness.

What about his other boats?

'My first mullet boat was a Logan-designed twenty-two-footer named *Rakoa*. I did a lot of work on her — she's in the National Maritime Museum.'

Tusi Tala was another boat to come into Barry's hands. He needed a docile craft to cruise the Gulf, and his strong attraction to old boats led him to the 32-foot beauty from the Logan crop of 1904. After a thirteen-year love affair, Barry has just parted with her and he now owns a 32-year-old Lidgard keeler, *White Heather*, which proudly swings from a mooring on the upper reaches of the Waitemata Harbour near his Beach Haven home.

'Look at this.' He waves at the view. 'You can't see a house in any direction.' It's true — you can't.

I notice a dinghy parked at the bottom of the walkway leading to his small jetty. 'I have to pick the tides to get out, but that's a small price to pay.'

Barry Simmonds is another who has contributed to the preservation of the classic boats conceived by the great boat-builders around the turn of the century. But he never won the coveted Lipton Cup — third, within 30 seconds of the winner, was the best he managed. However, Barry's eldest son, Mark, went on to win this trophy four times in a new mullety, limited edition.

That's history now, as is *Tao Tane* herself, frozen in time in a great photo on Barry's wall — one of the greatest mullet boats of all time.

Chris Smith

The Sporting and Dramatic Review, a news-sheet of the late 19th century, proclaimed: 'Moana has the Logan finish and that speaks for itself.'

Moana was a 5-rater built for the Wilson brothers, of Wilson and Horton newspaper fame, and first dipped her bow into the Waitemata swell in November 1895.

When she easily won her class in the 1896 Auckland Anniversary Regatta, the New Zealand Herald, usually reserved in its praise of its proprietors' yachting exploits, reported 'she is far and away the fastest boat of her size in Auckland'. And so she remained for three more seasons.

If you take the ferry to Auckland's North Shore, just off the Devonport Wharf you can see the sleek, almost unaltered Moana handsomely maintained, swinging on her mooring. She has passed through a select succession of owners since her launch, the most notable being the Millers, father and son. Both men were to become Commodore of the Royal New Zealand Yacht Squadron.

It was in 1969 that the name Smith became firmly linked with Moana. Returning home from an Anniversary Day race in a 14-foot Y-class skimmer, Peter Smith, with his wife and four sons, saw the mighty yacht thunder past under spinnaker.

It so happened owner Alf Miller had died and the boat was for sale. A family conference was hastily called. Could they even dream it? From their motley selection of yachts to one of the greatest of the Logan boats? Surely not.

Of such moments is history made. The Smiths bought Moana, despite finding her badly run down. Her fastenings were shot, she had dry rot round the rudder stock and she was leaking badly — to list just a few of her ailments.

Chris Smith, one of Peter's sons, recalls: 'One of my early jobs was to go aboard each day and pump out about fifty gallons [200 litres] of water. I did this for many years, sharing the duty occasionally with my mother and brothers.'

The upkeep and maintenance of Moana thus became a family affair, and so it continues to this day. Chris and Jenny Smith have become the primary care-givers over recent years, with Grant and Matthew less involved.

It's no secret that boats of Moana's vintage require many hours of maintenance and considerable finance to keep them in sailing, if not racing, trim. As Noel Holmes wrote in Century of Sail: 'Moana is an utterly graceful ship and I do not think the Smith family could have had a better tribute to their role in bringing her back to first rate condition.'

Hear, hear!

You'll see Moana, a supreme example of grace under sail in three centuries, regularly hammering down the Waitemata — a sight to quicken the pulse, I guarantee.

Fraser Smith

'**Is there** a story?' Each word is heavy with emphasis, as Kerry greets me at the door to the shed nestled under what has become known as the Albany Monument. Even New Zealand Post knows where to direct letters when they're addressed simply: 'Fraser Smith, The Monument, Albany, Auckland'.

'OK, it's been a few years since I started it,' agrees the amiable Fraser Smith. 'But I'll get her finished.'

The monument is a Chris Robinson-designed 45-footer — a big, beamy heavy-displacement launch perched high on the chocks on Fraser's property.

If there is one boat that has channelled the youth of New Zealand into a lifetime of boating, it would be the Z-class yacht, and Fraser came that route as well. In fact, as a youngster he sailed to Rangitoto and stayed the night. Considering the Zeddie is an open sailing dinghy, such an undertaking seems more foolhardy than adventurous.

Might some look upon Fraser's current preoccupation in the some way? Wayne Olsen, builder of many fine big boats, made the launch's hull and decks, and when the boat was delivered to Fraser about eight years ago, he asked, with prophetic insight: 'Do you know what you're getting yourself into?' Fraser certainly knows now — the 'finishing' has taken a little longer than expected.

I take a look at the vessel that has come to dominate this boating bloke's life. Solid, reliable, and has a decent range — she certainly scores well on those three counts. He brushes aside the jibe that she looks like the Waiheke ferry.

Kauri strip-planked, glassed inside and out — there's the strength he feels he needs to take him around New Zealand or maybe to Fiji. She's also powered by one of the greatest marine engines ever designed — the 6 L x B Gardiner — and can carry enough fuel to make it to the Islands.

The craftsmanship of the woodwork is awesome. His preferred interior finish is macrocarpa, which imparts a warm, traditional look. Autohelm has provided most of the toys on the space-age instrument cluster, and there are berths and stowage for plenty in a fastidiously designed below-decks. Already Fraser has turned down offers from passers-by who have caught a glimpse of the big boat from the highway just over the fence. It's a little hard to make out the precise lines of the boat under its tarpaulin shroud, but there's enough showing to get the picture.

'Not for sale,' is his reply, short and sweet.

It could be a classic, this boat. If Fraser can get the time away from his earth-moving and apartment-construction businesses to finish it, maybe I'll take up his offer to go for a ride.

'I don't care what other people think — I know she's a great boat.'

I'm with you, Fraser. I only await the invite.

Chad Thompson

Bressin Thompson is well-remembered at the Royal New Zealand Yacht Squadron. Not only because of his 61 years as a member of that august institution, nor the service he gave as Commodore, nor his beautiful Bailey-built-and-designed 43-footer, *Prize*, as legendary around the Hauraki Gulf as its proud owner. No, Bress had something more. He was of that generation of classic yachtsmen who forged what has since become the great New Zealand yachting legacy.

Bress' son, Chad, has extended the family contribution, advancing further the tradition of Corinthian yachting and taking over *Prize*.

'I was probably conceived on that boat,' he admits coyly. Chad's earliest memories are of the boat, and the amount of time spent on board.

Prize came to the Thompson family in the early 1940s. The 43-footer was commissioned by Auckland barrister and solicitor W.P. Endean, and hit the waters of the Waitemata in 1923. Her very name is the stuff of legend. HMS *Prize* was a submarine hunter during the First World War, and Lieutenant Commander Sanders of Takapuna won the Victoria Cross while serving on her, the only New Zealander in the Royal Navy to be awarded the ultimate military honour.

Chad remembers his early days on *Prize* as a mixture of racing and family cruising. She won the squadron points prize five summers in a row, from

1954 to 1958, a feat that hasn't been bettered to this day.

Chad's own entry into the world of competitive sailing was helped immensely by Ralph Roberts, who taught him tactics and the valuable art of getting the maximum out of a boat. Tom Dodson and Chris Dickson, two of the greats of New Zealand sailing, were his regular rivals in the early 1980s.

When Bress had a stroke in 1993, the boat that had been a family heirloom for so long passed into the care of Chad. Bress had ceased to race her seventeen years earlier, and Chad decided it was time for a rethink. As a temporary measure he had *Prize* spruced up for her seventieth birthday that year, but then gave her a major refit a couple of years later to put her back on the racing circuit. With the formation of the classic yacht association, with over 200 members and a calendar of events, *Prize* can once more wear her racing colours with pride.

Chad's occupation as a classic-yacht project manager and the attention he lavishes on the 77-year-old yacht complement each other perfectly.

Get onto the Waitemata one of these Saturdays and you may just get a glimpse of one of the flowers of New Zealand yachting under full sail. In *Prize* the era of the classic yacht is with us still.

Des Townson

Among the great designers, builders and yachtsmen who have helped make New Zealand the great yachting nation it is today, Des Townson is one of the few who should be crowned with laurel leaves. He chats easily while working deftly on his meticulously evolving Electron radio-controlled yachts in a basement workshop in Howick, southeast Auckland.

Models are what Des does these days, but his earlier achievements helped shape the course of New Zealand yachting history.

'I started as a motor-body-building apprentice, but didn't finish my time. I was never very good with my hands.'

The mind boggles at such understatement. Des Townson has designed and built some of the most beautiful yachts ever to grace New Zealand waters.

Des can remember when *Little Jim* and *Aramoana* were in the Gouldrey shed in Northcote, where the Auckland Harbour Bridge now hits the North Shore. He also recalls sailing in his father's mullet boat — the yacht that was to exert a lifetime's influence over him.

'I started boating like most kids. I remember being terrified sailing in frostbites. I sailed a P,' — he forgets to mention he won the Tanner Cup National Championship in 1950 — 'then Pennants and Q-class.'

It was then that a friend, John Peet, asked Des if he would draw a boat for him.

'A lot of guys were doing boats at the time, so I thought "Why not?"'

Thus began what can now be termed the Townson era. In 1956, Des designed the Zephyr, still a great boat today.

'It was the first one-design boat — built by one person using the same mould, thus practically guaranteeing equality of performance.'

Altogether, 219 Zephyrs came out of the Townson mould. And then there was *Moonlight*.

The 32-foot *Moonlight* was extraordinary. Peter Mulgrew campaigned in her against much larger opposition in the One Ton Cup in 1971 and almost made it.

'She certainly put me on the map. Everyone was talking about her.'

Des designed what he built and built what he designed. Pied Pipers, Mistrals, Starlings — a veritable stream of keel boats poured forth from the Townson workshop.

'I think there are about sixteen hundred of my boats out there now,' concludes Des.

He returns to his models — the glue is drying.

'Number six hundred and seventy,' he says, pointing to a bright-red one.

The Townson legend lives on.

Ken Warne

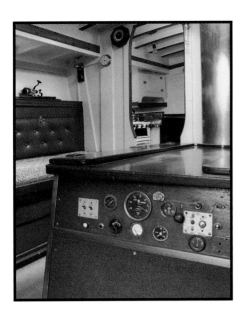

Elsewhere in this book is the story of Hugh Poole and how he found and restored his beloved X-class yacht, *Charade*.

Ken Warne's tale has a similar flavour.

It begins with Ken's father, Leon. The oldies will tell you the 1930s, 40s and 50s were the halcyon days of big-game fishing in the Bay of Islands, or anywhere in New Zealand for that matter. Leon was there with a boat named *Marline*, which he built in 1949 and launched in 1950 from his boatyard in Auckland's St Mary's Bay.

Ken, a builder by trade, helped with the construction.

When Leon retired, *Marline* was sold to people in Tauranga in 1958, and several subsequent owners added bits to her, including a fly bridge and a platform extending the stern deck.

Ken completely lost contact with the boat, and there the trail could have ended but for a chance encounter.

Driving across Panmure Bridge one day, Ken glanced down and, in the fleeting moment his eyes were off the road, he thought he recognised the familiar shape of *Marline*'s stern sticking out of Lane's shed.

'I wasn't certain, as she'd been altered over the years, but I did the back streets and found the shed. The owner was there, and we had a great laugh later when I showed him some old photographs. I also said that if he ever wanted to sell her he should give me a call.'

About a year later Ken did receive the call. The owner was finding *Marline* a handful as he grew older, so in 1990, after more than 30 years, the name Warne went back on the ownership papers.

On the outside, *Marline* looks today much the same as she has done for the past decade. Inside, it's a different story — remember she dates from 1949. Ken the builder spent countless hours working on the makeover. Don't ask him how long he took to return the woodwork to its original state after three decades of accumulated paint . . .

The boat on the piles in Auckland's Tamaki River looks a picture. Ken has completed the restoration with great skill, and the maintenance programme ensures that *Marline* always looks terrific.

'We cruise to the Bay of Islands,' says Ken, 'but maybe not as much as we should.'

There isn't the intense anticipation these days surrounding *Marline*'s presence in the Bay of Islands. But Ken's father, Leon, who fished with Zane Grey, would no doubt take great satisfaction from two facts. First, the boat he designed and built specifically for game fishing in the Bay of Islands returns periodically to the old haunts, and secondly she is back in the Warne family — probably for her remaining years.

Farquhar Wilkinson

'**I don't** know why so many musicians sail. Perhaps it's the quietness, an escape from all that noise they have to put up with when they're playing music.' Farquhar Wilkinson leans back in his cosy chair. It's mid-morning in Waikawa Bay, a fast-growing residential and retirement area, a stone's throw from Picton, attracting a lot of folk from Wellington.

'When a friend of mine, Bob Burch, another retiree from the New Zealand Symphony Orchestra suggested I look at this place when my playing days were over, I thought he was mad. But it's everything I want. We're totally sold on it.'

If you have been to listen to the NZSO over the past 50 years, you will have seen Farquhar. He was the one with the shock of wavy hair sitting in the front of the cellos, and for many years was the leader of that section. A stalwart, he's been there since day one, from the beginnings of the orchestra in 1953.

The NZSO in the 1980s had a hard core of boaties: Charlie Mountford, Chris Salmon, Bob and Farquhar. They were mostly trailer sailer guys, but when Farquhar had got used to the idea of Waikawa Bay and started looking around for a boat, he was advised to get a keeler.

'I'd chartered boats in the Sounds before, but never owned one,' he says.

An extensive search throughout the country ended in Auckland, and after careful consideration he purchased a 26-foot Tracker keel boat. He trucked it to Wellington and began putting it through its paces before he retired. When D-day arrived and it was adios to a lifetime of constant practice, rehearsals, travelling and concerts, the Tracker and Farquhar headed for the Marlborough Sounds (with Barbara, of course).

'The boat's just right for me and the Sounds. I love taking people out, and through my membership of Waikawa Bay Boating Club I race occasionally.'

No small affairs, these Wednesday-night races attract up to 45 boats, a good fleet in any port.

Farquhar has developed a lifestyle to die for: a piece of the best real estate in New Zealand, the ideal boat, an occasional game of golf and a schedule that couldn't be more different from the rigorous demands of the concert routine.

Does he play any music now? 'Not at all. I thought I would miss it terribly, but two years ago I sold my cello. I haven't played a note since.'

His love of music is still evident, now in the name of his boat, *Portamento*. 'It's a musical term, meaning when a string player slides his finger up the string while playing . . . I thought adagio, presto, largo and so on, but *Portamento* was perfect.'

The only other concession to music now is a partly finished harpsichord this bloke is building in his shed. I ring back an hour later. He's not there. Gone sailing. On *Portamento* . . .

He'll be back some time. Sounds time.

Malcolm Wilkinson

Malcolm Wilkinson always made model yachts as a youngster despite the fact he wasn't all that interested in sailing. 'I was in the Sea Scouts and got out a bit on Sydney Harbour, but that's about all.' He's still not really interested, but sailing model boats — that's an entirely different matter. He makes replica radio-controlled model yachts that are really something special. 'It was the launch of John Bolland's boat that got me interested.'

The occasion prompted him to hunt down literature on the subject, and he walked out of a bookstore with the weighty tome, *Fifty-three Boats to Build*. There was just one problem: these were real, full-sized boats. Solution: scale them down. 'I always wanted to be a boat-builder, but for various reasons that didn't happen, so now I just build models.'

They are beautifully made — exquisite, in fact. But most striking is what you don't see when you look at them. Remarkably, Mal uses the same methods as a builder of full-size boats. Each of the ribs is individually bent to shape. Each plank is laid individually — no strips of plywood are pencilled over in these beauties. Then, when that is done and everything fastened by treenails — tiny wooden pegs that are glued in — it's covered up so you can't see it. So why such painstaking attention to authenticity?

'Simple. When you're doing that, you're doing nothing else.'

Mal is a cabinet-maker by trade, and to say his work is extraordinary is a huge understatement: it's spectacular. His main client is an American millionaire, who buys most of what he makes. He works alone — sketching, copying, improvising and carving to a standard that truly has to be seen to be believed. The brass lion on the Lion Breweries building is his; so too a wooden pattern from which the replicas of the America's Cup were made in 1987.

The same degree of craftsmanship and attention to detail are evident in his boats. All the fittings — and there are plenty — are made by hand, the hull and decks are kauri and mahogany, the rigging authentic. And everything works.

'My big boat is called *Saltheart Foam Follower*. She's a model of an American Coaster design of 1914.'

Malcolm belongs to a group of enthusiasts who take vessels to the Onepoto pond on Thursdays. 'We call ourselves the "Ancient Mariners". We have a bit of fun, and the occasion's a great relaxation.'

A third boat is on the board. 'She's a Herreschoff, based on the 58-foot ketch *Tioga*. I'll do it the same way — individual planks, stringers and ribs.' All to be hidden from view eventually, I imagine.

Mal is modest about his exceptional ability, but whether he is finishing off a replica Louis XIV dresser or a model yacht, the meticulous precision of his work is there to see . . . Well, most of it, anyway.

Robbie Williams

It's one of those exceptional Napier days — flat calm, brilliantly sunny, warm — as Robbie Williams sculls the dinghy out to *Felicity*, on piles in the harbour basin.

'Good to see the art of sculling isn't dead,' I mumble as we glide alongside. Sculling was something I could never master myself.

Felicity — is she a topsail schooner or a brigantine? The technical difference has always been subtle, and whatever Robbie decides she is, it's OK by me.

Some facts are less contentious. She's a 35-footer from a design by John Atkin, from Connecticut, and was built of kauri and white pine (the spars are Oregon) by Robbie and Val in Tamatea, a suburb of Napier, in 1988.

Robbie's life at sea reads like a rundown of New Zealand's maritime history. He started out on the Union Steamship Company colliers, then joined *Rangatira*. He did time on the Cook Strait scows, and was even harbourmaster in Motueka for a couple of years.

Felicity is a well-used boat. Her coal range provides warmth on a cold winter day, while her accommodation is functional without being flashy. *Felicity* is copper fastened.

'There are five thousand, six hundred rivets on board,' Robbie tells me. 'Val knows, she's counted them.'

Two lesser features Robbie points out straight away. First, the drawer pulls are from that gallant barque *Pamir*. How Robbie came by them I don't inquire. Second, the sofa buttons are from his father's uniform.

'He was a skipper on the Anchor Line,' he explains.

Then Robbie points out another of *Felicity*'s unique features — her sails. They're all hand-sewn. I examine them and marvel at the handiwork, the extent and perfection of the stitching. It must have taken countless weeks to finish them to this standard.

When they demolished the old St Pat's Cathedral in Napier, pieces of it went hither and yon. Robbie acquired the doorstep and fashioned it into a serviceable rudder.

'We've made her so she can be sailed well by just three or four people,' he explains. And today he and Val prove the point as they head out for a Sunday off the coast. Not enough air, really, but it's such a great day.

As I drive out of town I see *Felicity* well out to sea, all sails set. A brigantine, I conclude — or maybe a topsail schooner.

It doesn't matter. She's a magnificent sight whatever she is.

Don Wright

It is with obvious pride that Don Wright exhibits his blazer, removing it from its protective wrapping with great care. The breast pocket tells the story: date — 1950; sport — surf life-saving; rank — New Zealand representative.

The silver fern has always been special, but I see straight away that this is extra special. Don was 35 when he qualified for the national team, the high point of a period in this exceptional 84-year-old's life that he recalls with particular affection. 'I was pretty handy on a surf ski. We made them in those days. Plenty of energy and enthusiasm but no money.'

Handy is exactly the right word to describe Don Wright. Big, knocked-about labourer's hands, and proud of them. 'I had five trucks at one stage. Worked for Henderson Pollard for thirty years.'

Handy with a set of tools as well. *Kawerau*, designed and built by Don himself, may be New Zealand's most famous surf boat. She doubled as a fishing boat, doing heavy duty in that capacity off the west coast near Auckland, and her unique (for a boat) source of power — a Dodge truck motor — gave her an impressive turn of speed.

'We used to catch and sell the fish and crayfish to support the Piha surf life-saving club. Couldn't do that these days.'

The conversation in the comfortable Remuera house Don built about the time of the Second World War (I'm sitting next to a nostalgic party piece — a La Gloria radiogram) is sprinkled with the names of famous — some might say infamous — New Zealanders: Tom Pearse, Fred Allen, Laurie Davidson, the Woodroofe boys, Andy Donovan.

On the east coast Don had the 36-foot *Lady Shanler*, a Hacker design from the United States. Built from Mangawhai Heads kauri Don milled himself in 1959, she took shape in a Penrose shed and hit the water in 1963.

'We made fifteen or sixteen fishing trips to the Barrier every year in her, no matter what the weather. She was a great sea boat.'

He riffles through a pile of photographs, recounting facts, times, places, and mates now gone. This maritime veteran has remarkable recall, his sparkling eyes lighting up as he darts from one yarn to another, the legacy of 70 years on the sea.

What of *Kawerau* today? She's lying in a paddock on Norfolk Island, quietly fading away. *Lady Shanler*, on the other hand, is as sound as ever, now working out of Tutukaka.

So much to tell, so little time to tell it. The first aqualungers in New Zealand, the first wet-suit importers — the stories roll on.

Don stands and repacks his blazer. It's only then I notice the small badge on the lapel: 'Patron Piha SLC'. Seventy-five years a man and boy dedicated to the sea. On it, in it and under it. Don Wright is a living legend of the truly good old days.

Peter Yeates

'**I think** it's an elemental, spiritual thing — a primal concept of man and boat. Warrior and transport — it's deep in the male psyche. Something to do with cavemen sitting astride floating logs; a bond between man and the sea.'

Different, I think.

I'm sitting below in *Iris*, Tim Yeates' boat, and propped in a corner, his father Peter Yeates is expounding his philosophy of men and their relationship with the sea. But what about the life and sea times of Peter himself?

'My first boat was made from a Spitfire fighter's drop tank. We simply cut a hole in it and there was a rudimentary canoe — highly unstable. My second was a tin hull. We attached an outrigger and went boating. Also highly unstable.'

Peter left those Folkstone beginnings and emigrated to New Zealand on the *Rangitane* in 1950.

'Many of the immigrant children who came by sea later became voyagers and very good sailors. New neuron circuits crackle into life when you migrate over the water.'

Peter has owned many boats since. The 40-foot *Matarere* was one he particularly liked. She was a steam schooner built in 1906 by Charles Thomson.

'I sailed from Penang to New Zealand in 1971 with Wim Van Leeuwen aboard the *Boy Roel*. It was a four-month voyage exploring the Malay archipelago and the islands of Indonesia. A wonderful experience.

Tim's mother and I sailed to Mururoa on *Fri* in 1973. We spent a hundred and seventeen days blockading the French atmosphere nuclear tests.

A friend arrives and the conversation turns to old boats, sails, spars, fittings, and other people's stories.

But soon it's time to go, and for the first time I see *Waipapa*, the 19-footer Peter arrived in. Clearly she's seen better days, but oh, those classic lines!

'I bought her twenty-five years ago. She was built in 1894, and used for general cargo on the Kerikeri inlet and river. Later she held a contract, for fifteen years, with the Education Department to transport local children from the inlets to the Opua School. I use her as a back-up boat. At the moment she's leaking like a punctured bucket,' Peter adds as he bails water from her. His main boat is *Mary Anne*. 'She went AWOL a fortnight back and was holed up on the Brampton Reef. We floated her off and she's presently under repair.'

Living up Waikare Inlet as he does, this 62-year-old pottery tutor uses boats like the rest of us use cars. Commuting by boat has become a way of life.

I'm still pondering the existential angst of the primeval spiritualisation as he guns the 2hp motor and *Waipapa* heads towards the shore, her owner cutting a Hornblower figure as he stands aft.

A very different sort of bloke.

Tim Yeates

As I look at *Iris* motoring slowly against the tide just off Opua Wharf, I can't imagine her as the scourge of the English Channel. But in her day that's what she was. She was put to sea by the 'revenuers' to blockade the pesky French trying to smuggle brandy ashore along the English coast.

'She was fast in her day,' says owner Tim Yeates. 'She had a huge rig and could run down most ships in a good breeze.'

This is hard to figure when you take a close look. In the first place, she weighs about 50 tons. Secondly, she has a beautiful broad bow, characteristic of the Bristol Channel cutters, the ships that took pilots out to meet the square riggers as they arrived from the four corners of the globe. These hard men of the sea would endure days, even weeks, out in the rough water of the channel, waiting. There was no radio back then to warn of an arrival, and a ship might appear at any time.

Down below, in the sailors' quarters, there is a strong sense of that era 120 years ago, when *Iris* offered far less in the way of comfort than she does today.

Registered in 1864, *Iris* was built of teak and English oak, in the days when an adze was used to finish the curves (of which evidence can still be seen in the stern timbers). She must be one of the oldest vessels sailing in New Zealand today.

After *Iris* had been decommissioned following the First World War, she was sold to a lord as a private yacht, and went on to spend 60 years as a houseboat on the English waterways. In 1986 she was brought to New Zealand by an adventurous family, a trip that took ten years. Then, after she had been lying idle in the Bay of Islands for a while, Tim approached the owner to ask about renting her.

'I needed somewhere to live,' he explains. 'I'm twenty-six now and haven't lived on land since I was eighteen. It's a long story, but I ended up buying her three years ago.'

The dedicated effort that has to go into the repair and transformation of old boats to make them seaworthy again is enormous, but Tim has done a superb job. The decks look like a million dollars, and the great condition of the boat is evidence of Tim's concentrated work.

Tim has travelled the Pacific Islands in a little boat called *Jellicle*, and thinks of returning . . .

'I'd like to take *Iris* and maybe work her up there. Perhaps carry tourists — or timber. That's the long-term plan.'

For the moment, the 135-year-old revenue-chasing, pilot-cutter houseboat has a passionate owner in Tim Yeates. At a leisurely pace, she heads towards Marriot Island, Tim leaning on the extra-long spruce tiller — a picture of a bloke totally absorbed in his boat.

Bill McCarthy Author

The sea has always been part of Bill McCarthy's life. Born in Bluff, he grew up amidst the maritime clamour of the fishing industry. In the late 1960s, the success of Chris Bouzaid sparked Bill's interest in the sea as a source of leisure. Though he does not regard himself as a 'real' sailor, he has completed two trans-Tasman crossings by yacht, and has sailed with Peter Blake (now Sir) on *Ceramco*, *Lion N.Z.* and *Steinlager*. His working life, though, has been spent in radio and television, including five years as newsreader on TV One and ten years fronting 'The Boat Show'. He was formerly also Head of Sport for TVNZ. Bill now spends much of his time producing corporate and broadcast videos. He is married to concert pianist Rae de Lisle, with whom he shares his passion for classical music.

Brian Moorhead Photographer

Armed with a B.Sc in zoology, Brian Moorhead set out to become the next Jacques Cousteau. When that didn't happen, he turned to Plan B. This led him to a variety of occupations, including pharmaceutical marketing and research, international textile trading and eco-tourism. For the past fifteen years, though, Brian has been a full-time professional photographer, working largely in the advertising and commercial fields. Brian and his partner, Gaylene, run the Auckland-based Focus New Zealand Photo Library. When not behind the lens, Brian can be found slashing gorse and planting native trees on their recently purchased 47 acres of land at Muriwai. *Blokes & boats* is his first book.